More Praise for *Become*

"*Become* is an essential resource for those seeking to understand and harness their leadership potential. Hannum weaves theory, data, and storytelling to artfully craft a clear and compelling guide for the reader."

—**LISA DEANGELIS**, *Director of Center for Collaborative Leadership at University of Massachusetts Boston*

"'The essence of leadership is about people.' This sums it up for me. My friend, Mark Hannum guides us through analogies and stories that underscore what it takes to BECOME a true effective leader. This is a book that will be your go-to guidepost. A great read that is authentic and thought-provoking, inspiring, and impactful. Mark has created a must-read for leaders at all levels."

—**DARLENE SLAUGHTER**, *Chief People Officer, March of Dimes*

"Finally, Hannum has put together a resource that whimsically describes the true essence of leadership—all while simplifying the complexity around the term. In *Become*, Hannum inspires us to find our purpose and understand how our unique talents, skills and superpowers can drive innovation. A must-read for those who are and inspire to be in a position of influence at their companies."

—**AREZOO RIAHI**, *Senior Diversity & Inclusion Strategic Partner of Autodesk*

Jennifer
there would be
no book without you!
linkage is evolving
and changing every
day (in a good way)
thanks to your
leadership!
More to
Become!
Mark Hannum

BECOME

THE PATH TO
PURPOSEFUL
LEADERSHIP

MARK HANNUM

NEW YORK   CHICAGO   SAN FRANCISCO   ATHENS
LONDON   MADRID   MEXICO CITY   MILAN
NEW DELHI   SINGAPORE   SYDNEY   TORONTO

1 2 3 4 5 6 7 8 9   QVS   24 23 22 21 20 19

ISBN   978-1-260-45756-8
MHID   1-260-45756-7

e-ISBN   978-1-260-45757-5
e-MHID   1-260-45757-5

Library of Congress Control Number: 2019950588

McGraw-Hill books are available at special quantity discounts to use as premiums and sales promotions or for use in corporate training programs. To contact a representative, please visit the Contact Us pages at www.mhprofessional.com.

To Judy, Liz, and Stephanie

CONTENTS

FOREWORD

Why you lead determines how well you lead.

That statement is the title of an article I published in 2014 in *Harvard Business Review*, summarizing the findings of a study published in the *Proceedings of the National Academy of Sciences*. The study, led by Yale professor Amy Wrzesniewski, demonstrated that when people were driven to lead by a mix of external motivations (profit motive or personal ambition) and internal motivations (a sense of purpose), their leadership effectiveness was significantly less than those driven to lead by internal motivations alone. The message is clear: our very best leaders are not in it for themselves, but instead are internally driven toward resolving the needs and aspirations of others and of their organizations.

Yet despite the preponderance of evidence to the contrary, leader development enterprises still attempt to sell leader development strategies by attaching leadership ability to personal gain and riches. But Linkage, Inc.—with CEO Jennifer McCollum and author Mark Hannum, SVP, Research and Development—has redirected that broken paradigm.

At Linkage, leader development is about purpose, not perks. And that, more than any other single fact, underscores the value of this book. *Become: The Path to Purposeful Leadership* will be the leadership book that best defines internally driven leaders. Consider Linkage's five commitments:

1. Inspire (provide hope and inspiration toward a future vision)

2. Engage (offer opportunities to contribute and thrive at work)

3. Innovate (drive new thinking and creative freedom to create success)

4. Achieve (creates appropriate structure and clarity to achieve successful outcomes)

5. Become (lead with commitment, courage, compassion, and self-awareness)

These commitments make clear that in order to become great, a leader must be internally driven and purposeful. The purpose of *inspire* is to encourage others, the purpose of *engage* is to include others, the purpose of *innovate* is to chart new paths, and the purpose of *achieve* is to get consistent results toward organizational targets. Only in *become* is the leader preeminent, and even then, the objective is deep, internal growth, not some promised array of shallow, external rewards. Nowhere do the five commitments promise adoration, or fame, or material success.

Of course, this is not to imply that success does not follow purposeful leadership. It does—and much of Mark Hannum's research will prove just that. The Linkage Purpose Index, in fact, reveals a tight relationship between purposeful leadership and critically important business indicators such as financial performance, competitive differentiation, employee engagement, and a creative employee-driven net promoter score.

But the starting point is that purposefulness does not hinge on personal ambition or success; it is far more connected to the essence of leadership than that. Personal fulfillment is a step beyond personal ambition. Mark frees us from the tyranny of wanting too much, and by doing so, prepares us to receive much, much more.

Entire forests of trees have been cut down to provide paper for books on leadership. That's unfortunate, because if readers had come across *Become: The Path to Purposeful Leadership* first, they could have saved a lot of time. Mark is a management theorist whose long career has spanned training, organization development, executive coaching and leadership development, and he brings his considerable insights to bear on a book whose premise is unique, evidence-based, and fundamentally attached to the sense of purpose that drives so many of our best leaders.

As lucidly presented as it is, this isn't a book to be treated casually—but you will get a strong return on your investment of time. I placed demands on this book, and Hannum met them. You should do the same. Not only will you begin to think differently about leadership, but you'll feel prompted to reconsider the way you lead. Mark Hannum's book will help many leaders to *Become*.

—*Tom Kolditz, Founding Director,*
Ann & John Doerr Institute for
New Leaders, Rice University

PREFACE

I am a leadership consultant. My colleagues and I at Linkage, Inc., help organizations put the appropriate systems, tools, and processes in place, to improve the quality and effectiveness of their leaders. Linkage is an international leadership development firm focused on helping Fortune 1000 companies build their leaders— and ultimately, the overall organization, resulting in better outcomes for increasing revenues and profit. We have been providing the tools to help leaders improve on leaders for 25 years, creating a huge database of information on leadership skills and qualities. While I try not to change the company's fundamental values or strategies in the process, oftentimes I find myself pulled into a redefinition and clarifying process to make the strategy clearer and easier to implement.

At its core, leadership consulting first entails making certain that each leader is the best possible version of himself or herself. Second, leadership consulting involves making sure that the leadership collective have a similar way of practicing the art of leadership. Warren Bennis, a thought leader in this specialty and a former

Linkage, Inc., board member, referred to this as herding cats. As soon as you felt that everyone was on board and aligned, someone would go rogue and the puzzle would need to be rearranged. This kind of work requires one to constantly keep an ear to the ground as well as an eye open for the small tell-tale signs that someone is going in a different direction. Of course, sometimes a leader will go rogue because he or she simply misunderstands what is happening and why it is happening. This will usually result in executive coaching for that leader, or some other form of educational intervention. Third, leadership consulting means building basic organizational processes, such as leadership development workshops, succession planning systems, and enrichment education for leaders.

FROM CHIMPS TO EXECUTIVES

It is difficult to explain what I do. If I'm invited out to a party, it is much easier to stand in the corner and wait for the hors d'oeuvres to come around than it is to jump into the mix and have someone ask me what I do for a living. But inevitably people will ask me, and I will tell them that I help organizations to build their leaders. The stares I receive back are often the same reaction you get from your pet dog when she fails to understand what you are doing: the sideways cock of the head and the wide-open pupils. There usually isn't a great follow-up question. So I describe the basic, core strategies of leadership development.

"How did you get into that?" is usually the question back to me.

It was a happy accident. I grew up with an Irish Catholic mother who wanted me to be an Irish Catholic priest. I wanted to be an academic and an experimental psychologist. I left ideas of seminary behind and went to graduate school to train chimpan-zees how to communicate using sign language. After five years of research, my PhD evaporated with a major professor who left the university. Now I had to figure out how to make a living, and I certainly had no idea what I could be. I found a headhunting firm that did know what to do with me and found me a job working for a leadership development firm.

When a client of the leadership firm hired me, I went from being a consultant in leadership development to an underwriter at a commercial property and casualty insurance company. I learned the trade and also found myself working for some difficult leaders. In a commercial property and casualty insurance company, the job is to evaluate businesses to see whether or not they are insurable and at what price. Each file is a puzzle that has to be figured out. And I was very good at figuring out the puzzle because I focused on the leadership and management style of the potential insured.

Very quickly, I was promoted to trainer and then a developer of the training. I became the chief of staff to several high-ranking leaders. Finally, I jumped ship to join Hanover Insurance, a company that promised a new type of organization with a new type of leadership. As I progressed in learning about insurance, I also became enamored with what I was learning about organizations and leadership from Hanover's CEO, William J. O'Brien, and his reincarnation of the company.

At Hanover, I had started on the business side and I ended up on the organizational development and training side. As I tried to find my way in the home office, I became attached to the CEO's major project with MIT's Center for Organizational Learning. I got to work with the faculty at the Sloane School of Business, a gaggle of young PhD students, and some of the best organizational development practitioners in the country from companies such as Ford Motor, General Motors, the Walt Disney Company, Analog Devices, and In-Focus, as well as a host of technology companies that eventually got acquired and merged into what is now Silicon Valley. I learned the difficult skill of systems thinking. I also learned how to consult. Most importantly, I was learning leadership. I was not just learning how to be a leader by leading, but these experiences put me behind the curtain examining leadership with skilled, thoughtful practitioners who, by and large, became some of the gurus of leadership in the world.

GETTING PAST MY AMBIVALENCE WITH LEADERSHIP

This brings me to the real irony of this story, not one that I often share at the cocktail parties. You see, by the time I got to Hanover, I wasn't a big fan of leadership in general or specific leaders I had worked for in my short career. I grew up in the sixties. I remember the assassination of three gigantic leadership figures: John F. Kennedy, Martin Luther King Jr. and Robert F. Kennedy. All three were still in the process of telling us who they were, what they wanted to accomplish, and why they wanted to accomplish it. All three were still very young men. All were flawed in some ways, focused and engaging in other ways. I watched all three lose their lives, I was also cognizant that we didn't lose the dreams they left us.

It also was easy to see many other leadership failures in the 60s and 70s: failures in the conduct of war, in the management of public protests on college campuses (not just Kent State, but certainly highlighted by it), and in the handling of domestic terrorism, as well as criminal conduct in the White House. More local to my hometown, the largest business in town—a factory—closed, and the employee pensions were stolen. Employees' healthcare was taken away. My friends and their families moved away so the parents could find work. My classmate's mother, whose husband had lost his job in the factory closing, died in childbirth because of poor care. My heroes in the local high school returned from Vietnam, and I served as the altar boy at their funerals. Leadership always seemed to be attached to something negative.

It wasn't all negative, of course. Even as some people predicted the fall of civilization, the Beatles were producing sounds that were making a positive difference in all of our lives. I got to see the future when my family went to the New York World's Fair. I started to understand the words and poetry of Bob Dylan. I watched as NASA thrilled us again and again and ultimately had a man walk on the moon. I saw Disney World.

I learned a lot about leadership: organizing people and keeping them interested through the drudgery, innovating experiments, and dealing with the administration and the media. I worked for consultants who theorized how to create great organizations but couldn't manage their own. I jumped into the difficult world of financial services and learned that people who could manage the money got the leadership jobs, even though leadership is about people. I worked with leaders who were ineffective, even toxic. I worked with leaders who lacked character, training, and discipline. I grew cynical and skeptical of leadership. I doubled down on that cynicism by being a clunky but overly ambitious leader myself.

I also learned that there are great leaders. Leaders who spelled out a direction, cared deeply for the people that they worked with, knew how to organize people to succeed, and knew how to pull the levers of power and use symbolism. These people had leadership chops. They certainly had the ability to pull people together to accomplish a goal. They had a knack for communicating and inspiring. They were the very definition of courageous and bold. As I came to know these leaders, my cynicism softened. My discernment deepened.

STUDYING LEADERSHIP

Leadership is not one skill but a demanding complex of skills. And what I know now is that leaders are the individuals who set goals *that we all want to achieve, shared goals.* Leaders also have a positive impact on people and situations. I've learned that effective leaders, the ones I would follow, are elegant: simple, humble, focused, and positive. The good leaders I have worked with over the years have not changed this belief, nor have the bad leaders.

When I finally got deep into organizational theory and leadership at Hanover, I had the benefit of working with a generous and pioneering set of thought leaders who worked with us and our CEO, William J. O'Brien. Most notable were Peter Senge, the author of *The Fifth Discipline*; Chris Argyris of Harvard University, the consultant's consultant; Russell Ackoff, author of *Management f-Laws*—the flaws in both leaders and the practices of leadership that get embedded in organizations; Donella Meadows, who helped conceptualize the archetypes of systems thinking and personally mentored me; Henry Mintzberg, the management theorist; Edgar Schein of group process and organizational culture fame; and Marvin Weisbord of Future Search.

While they probably don't all remember me, I remember their streak of cynicism that kept me off balance and the touch of optimism that kept me intrigued. It was at Hanover that leadership became a subject for me as opposed to an object. I studied the subject of leadership. I read book after book on the subject, and passed up on many more.

The next big iteration of my engagement with leaders and leadership came over 15 years of consulting to leaders trying to build leadership systems, strategies, and organizations. Through building competency models of leadership to building leadership systems for companies to working with leaders to transform their organizations, I learned even more. First, we are all leaders: In any organization trying to elevate itself, we all lead the change. Some more visibly than others. Some with words, and others with actions. We all want to be engaged and to be a major contributor to the change's success. We all want to find the creative or innovative idea that turns the key. And we all want to be a part of the team, the group, or the function that makes it work. Second, leaders have goals— goals that resonate with whole communities of people. Goals transform the current state. Goals do this by inspiring people to act and do things differently. Goals are not critiques of the past; they are dreams of what you want to become.

Martin Luther King Jr.'s famous "I have a dream" leadership speech was not a protest. It was very simple and elegant. It was very aspirational. It wasn't a fantasy. And it left us dancing. Leaders with great goals pushed past all the conflict and tension, removed any doubt about self-interest, and dissolved the messiness and noise of the current state. I met Donella Meadows through the Center for Organizational Learning, and she taught me that "great goals change everything." Nothing has proved more true to me about leadership. The opposite has also proved true: Leaders without goals have always shown themselves over time to be the definition of empty suits.

REDEFINING LEADERSHIP

By 2011 I was working at Linkage and began a project to update and reconceptualize Linkage's approach to leadership. Linkage had been founded in 1988 by Phil Harkins, an entrepreneur. In relatively short order, Phil had established a relationship with Warren Bennis, the leading academic involved in the research of leadership. Linkage's leadership point of view was a derivation, with Warren's blessing, of his research and thinking. Our association and relationship with Warren gave our leadership model a certain status and distinction in the world of leadership experts. Warren was one of the first researchers to put leadership under both quantitative and qualitative analysis. He led the way when it came to focus, energy, and wisdom. Warren died, and a number of research studies and findings were starting to tear at the fabric of leadership thinking in general. Having a sponsor with the status of Warren Bennis has both positive and negative impacts. Changing our point of view would mean moving away, ostensibly, from Warren's point of view and the uniqueness and distinctiveness that Warren's work bestowed on us. Moving my peers out of their comfort zone would be no small task. One night in a mediocre restaurant over bad burgers, I asked my peers if they thought we had leadership right. I mentioned *Moneyball* and Billy Beane and the certainty of baseball experts who had baseball all wrong. I mentioned the Kahneman and Tversky studies on experts and how experts were wrong as often as novices. I mentioned the Malcolm Gladwell book *Blink* and how it explained our unconscious motives for doing certain things and deciding things certain ways. My peers expressed their certainty that we had it right. They were captivated with our Bennis model of leadership, even with the shadows being cast by hundreds of studies and countless researchers.

So I did what I do. I read books on leadership. I live in a virtual garden of leadership experts, academics, and scholars, so I went to every lecture I could find. I constructed a foundational set of ideas and brought it to my peers. They saw value in my theory and my hypotheses. We engaged a team, and we did the research to prove out those hypotheses that there was a more impactful way to lead. We analyzed the 360-degree data of more than 100,000 leaders we had on file from more than 20 years. We looked at the competency models and at the hundreds of interviews we did building the many leadership models for our clients. We interviewed academic and corporate experts in leadership and leadership development. We assembled a large number of case studies, studying how each became the leader that they did. We found our way inch by inch to what we now call Purposeful Leadership. We tested the concepts with our clients and with experts. We refined. We simplified. We made it into an elegant concept. Most importantly, we made it learnable.

Leadership seems to have more facets than a diamond, with yet another theory, another theorist, and another key behavior. It seems like the world of leadership cannot even figure out how to write a comprehensive and readable book on the subject. The conversation about leadership was *not* working, and it was my time to enter the conversation. I'm building on the many leadership books that represent the insights of the last half century.

ACKNOWLEDGMENTS

Any significant endeavor involves more than one person, but when one person sits down and ends up documenting the work, particularly in book form, that person will get an undue amount of the credit. *Become: The Path to Purposeful Leadership* is more than the work of just one person. This book is an outcome of the work and thought of many.

Let's be real. When purposeful leadership was a mere aspiration, it also represented an inspiration to the lives of everyone at Linkage. I had made several internal presentations on what I was discovering, and we had multiple energetic conversations about the meaning of it all. But it wasn't really catching fire. It wasn't until a new CEO came to Linkage, Matt Norquist, that we started to move the needle on this project. Not only was Matt a supporter and a champion, but he brought real quantitative skills to the project, compounding our insights and the meaning behind them. There would be no purposeful leadership as it exists today without Matt and the members of the executive team at the time: Reed Parker, Ron Porter, and Dana Yonchak.

Additionally, there were many people who contributed to the development of purposeful leadership. Charley Morrow and Kael Alberghini were statistical wizards analyzing the 360-degree feedback data from multiple instruments that Linkage has used to measure leadership over the years. Their role has been ably taken over by Nada Hashmi, Assistant Professor of Information Systems Technology, Operation and Information Management at Babson College. Sam Lam and Desley Khew from Linkage's Singapore operation, along with their colleagues, gave our research a major shot in the arm and provided critical validation at an inflection point in our initiative. Many consultants, including Donald Auger, Sarah Bettman, Susan Brady, Paula Butte, Stu Cohen, Briana Goldman, Bernardus Holtrop, Susie Kelleher, Shirley Milgrom, Laura Stone, David Vaughn, and Madelyn Yucht, contributed thought leadership. I'm also immensely grateful to our project manager, Kirsten Ruf, for being willing to go on the wild ride with us, being the voice of common sense and just being all around awesome. I will also be forever in the debt of Rachael Marangu, the product manager for leadership at Linkage. I would say things, and Rachael would say them back to me and give me new understanding of my own thoughts and words. Lauren Rodriguez did an amazing literature search and bibliography while in the midst of a life-changing move to Ireland. Rick Pumfrey played no small part in helping to create the copyright on the term "purposeful," which was a journey all by itself. And finally, a very special mention to Devon Brown who helped to create the Purposeful Leader 360 Degree Assessment with Donald Auger, facilitate the education of our staff on purposeful leadership, and generally provide key thinking and research assistance.

Since its debut, purposeful leadership has been incorporated into a number of client interventions and an academy at Linkage. Turning a concept into activities that inspire and teach people how to lead is no small task. Led by Kristen Howe and Shirley Milgrom, a team made up of Angela Hicks, David Vaughn, Stephen Monk, Alexander Martin, Lizzette Lima, managed to surpass all expectations in designing and developing a fantastic experience.

Maria Howard and Sarah Breigle and their marketing team, as well as the key members of our design function: Lori Hart, Teresa Raithel, Amy Kimball, and Brianna MacGregor, have the unenviable job of promoting purposeful leadership, our academy, and this book with their graphics, their marketing copy, their publicity efforts, and their editing. I am incredibly grateful to them for all that they do. It is also hard to imagine the day-to-day job of making purposeful leadership work for clients, and Sarah Dayton, Scott Gavriel, and Kristin Barrett have supported and shaped how we work with clients since the very beginning.

Two clients in particular were more than generous in their support and their belief in purposeful leadership. Lynn Wooten, who is currently the David J. Nolan Dean at Cornell University, Dyson School of Applied Economics and Management, and Frauke Harnischfeger, who is currently leading HR with the African Development Bank Group. Without the support and guidance of these two individuals, no progress would have been made with purposeful leadership; it would have been a perpetual possibility. This is in no way meant to downplay the role that a great many other clients played in my development as a consultant and as a leadership coach. Tom Goemaat, Bill Hughes, and Susan Ehrlich at Shawmut Design and Construction, Mike Casey and Kim Fields at JM Family, and Mark Van Tine and his leadership team at Jeppesen were as influential in my life as I was in theirs. It's a debt I can never repay.

Nor would I have ever gotten to where I am without the help, input, feedback, and occasional kick that so many great leadership experts have given me over the years. Their influence is documented in the pages of this book. Many are no longer with us, some may not remember me, while others are still making their presence known to my thinking every day. It's not just leaders who need formation.

When Matt moved on, Jennifer McCollum arrived on the scene as our new CEO in 2018. The idea for this book was all over the map. Jennifer approached me and asked if I would take it over and make it mine. I was willing and ready to do that. She has been unwavering in her support of the book, its message, and all its twists and turns. This was my first book that was aimed at a mainstream audience and represented a big learning curve for me. I was ably assisted by Candi Cross in putting together the proposal and the manuscript. I was also assisted by multiple proof readers: Jaye Chen in particular invested lots of time in helping me work on the manuscript.

This is where a great team needs to engage and support you, and McGraw-Hill and Donya Dickerson led that team. Her belief in the message of the book overwhelmed and supported its production. She "got it." She and her team were invaluable in shaping the structure and the narrative of the book. Needless to say, they were also key in correcting my Oxford commas, my way too frequent use of colons, my erratic use of apostrophes, and my overuse of quotations.

When push came to shove and the manuscript needed a final polish, Stephen Isaacs was Donya's choice to help me finish the project. His guidance, improvements, challenges, and reassurance *were* the guidance that was needed.

There are, of course, many other people to whom I am indebted for their guidance, support, and partnership over the course of my career: Linkage's founder, Phil Harkins, for one, and David Giber, for another. But the depth of my gratitude can never repay the debt I owe Jill Ihsanullah for our partnership for the last two decades.

I've been very fortunate that she decided to put so much time and energy into the project called Mark. Jill has shored up and bolstered this project in so many ways, it is literally impossible to keep track of her influence. Her scholarship, expertise, and energy are all over purposeful leadership.

But all of this would not have been possible without the support of my wife, Judy. I still don't think she understands that playing the same five chords in a row on my guitar for 20 minutes or pacing endlessly for 45 minutes at a time is actually writing, and she may have a point. She gave me the space to do this book project as well as purposeful leadership. As my insights grew and my opinions got more emphatic, I could count on her to bring me down to earth and restore my compassion. She has listened to all my stories of leaders and leadership, and she still laughs at the parts she is supposed to laugh at. That is how you build a marriage that lasts 42 years.

Our daughters, Elizabeth and Stephanie, both grown and living the life of leaders in the real world, have had to suffer through small bites of my "coaching." Fortunately they seek out their mother more than myself. Unfortunately, they also had to soldier on during multiple family vacations when I stayed behind and worked on either purposeful leadership or this book. They have unwittingly taught me much about learning to lead. They have no idea how much insight I gather from overhearing the conversations they have with Judy about work, leading, and managing. I'm grateful to be watching them grow and progress in an era when women can be thought of as equal, but I'm equally troubled and deeply motivated by watching them go through situations where that is not true. Though Purposeful Leadership and this book are about being effective as a leader, they are also about restoring trust in leaders as fair, compassionate, courageous, and inclusive individuals. We still have a long way to go, and my hope is this book will make a difference.

INTRODUCTION: WHY PURPOSE?

I think the truth of the matter is, people who end up a "first" don't actually set out to be first. They set out to do something they love and it just so happens that they are the first to do it.
> —Condoleezza Rice, U.S. Secretary of State (2005–2009)

WHY DO WE HAVE LEADERS?

What is the value of a leader? What purpose does a leader really serve in a group of people? What does a leader provide to a group of people that cannot be obtained elsewhere? How does a leader create a distinct advantage for that group?

Leadership is not so easily understood; if there is a code to leadership effectiveness, it is constructed with a vocabulary of thoughts, actions, or behaviors. In all likelihood, leadership has developed in many organizations without a written code, evolving over time with a tacit set of understandings about how to lead.

1

That is not to say that written codes don't exist. The U.S. Army and the U.S. Navy, just to name two examples, have written down their codes for leading over the decades. They have improved their codes from time to time as technology and the rules governing armed conflict have evolved. A number of organizations in the world have also written down or created specific principles or axioms for their leadership. They've also improved them over time, while adjusting to changes in the global economy, technology, generations, and the organization's values. But overall, most of these organizations have probably experienced a certain amount of unwritten evolutionary change in their code as practitioners have pummeled the rules of the game to improve their own position, finding what works more expedient than what is understood. And a fair amount of knowledge is lost from generation to generation as the verbal and visual nature of the transfer of the knowledge it takes to lead is handed from one leader to the next.

Some organizations thrive on the lack of leadership rules of the road. These organizations may actually grow and prosper on the anarchy created by hundreds of leaders who all do things their own way. These organizations have a kind of leadership Wild West and a sorting mechanism that eliminates ineffective leaders with either extreme quickness or maybe extreme slowness. When organizations don't have leadership rules of the road or principles of leadership, sorting out good leaders from bad can be difficult. Without a written code of leadership, standards can be quickly altered to accommodate whatever is happening in the moment. Once an organization has its leadership road rules, the organization's credibility and trustworthiness depend on upholding those standards. This can present a range of problems that might be inconvenient to deal with: the bad leader who gets results, the exceptional person who does not get results, or the leader who might trample over process to get the results.

When we analyzed Linkage's data from 20 years of 360-degree feedback, we had to find a substitute for leadership value; in other words, to sort leaders into categories of effectiveness, we needed to have criteria. We needed to understand, based on what we had in our database, who was considered effective and ineffective. When we based value on the percentage of fives (the highest ranking you can get) a participant received and then correlated the behaviors to effectiveness, we found a very definitive answer: Highly valued leaders drive the organization through vision, strategy, and goals. The value of a leader is in his or her capability to create, to articulate, to energize and align people, and to actualize the aspirations (i.e., vision, mission, strategy, goals, and objectives) of the organization. In other words, leaders lead around a purpose. Leaders own the goals, the aspirations of the organization. They don't need to always create them, but they need to own them and create the path and the plan to achieve them.

As much as we wanted to believe completely that we had found the answer, the ease with which we discovered this insight made us wary. Our academic research had not been this definitive. There were plenty of popular authors and gurus on leadership who never mentioned this aspect of leadership. What was it about this key piece of data that was at once surprising and yet validating?

We empaneled a group of leadership experts and posed the question of value to them. Time and time again, we heard some variation on the basic idea that the leader is the owner or the creator of the strategy or the direction of the company, the function, the team and its goals. The words that were used were sometimes vague and sometimes confusing, but still had a similar trajectory. Leaders were said to be the people who create the organization's goals. Others said that leaders were the ones who articulated and communicated what everyone felt was the shared goal. Leaders ultimately owned the goal-setting process in the organization and its outcomes. To cite the most articulate expert of the group, "Leaders have a certain quality about them; they understand why they want to lead. They have a strong sense of something that they need to accomplish." Some said this in almost spiritual terms. Some conveyed this in puzzled terms as if they themselves didn't understand what they were telling us. Some advocated the idea and tried to sell us on it. Leaders have a personal sense of purpose. Leaders constantly make choices, and the best leaders are guided by their own sense of purpose and how it aligns with the organizational mission. The best leaders are purposeful in where they are leading, and they are purposeful in how they get there. A theme was definitely becoming clear.

Let me say this: Not everyone used the word "purposeful" or "purpose." We heard every possible combination and permutation of the term: "intention," "motive," "plan," etc. We heard variations like, "They are the most mindful person in the company." We heard other variations about leaders having a dream or some ideal in their head. What we heard is that effective leaders have a personal sense of purpose that they have merged with the organizational mission in a unique and dynamic brew.

THE UNEXPECTED LEADER

This idea of a purpose-driven leader caused me to reflect on the strong leaders I've observed in my own life. As a young adult, I moved with my spouse and young daughters to a small town in Massachusetts to be closer to our parents. While the town we moved into was considered one of the best in the state for income, jobs, education quality, standard of living, and quality of life, it was dominated by senior citizens who voted down anything that did not directly benefit them or lower their tax burden. The schools were good but rapidly decaying. Teachers were getting frustrated with their pay and needing to buy supplies out of their own pockets. We had no playgrounds and just a few ball fields mostly for the boys to use. Some of us focused on what we could do, and we did it. But I fondly remember the auto mechanic in town who had children of his own, and he started to talk to people about a playground for our kids. He got people excited. He set the goal and became the instantaneous symbol around the playground idea. With no formal training or experience, he became the leader. He garnered some seed money from the town government in a town meeting. He knocked on the door of a famous architect who lived in town and asked if he would design the playground. The architect declined because he was a tennis court architect. However, he recommended someone in the Carolinas who specialized in children's playgrounds.

The auto mechanic, our leader, drove south and knocked on that architect's door. They discussed the need, the process, and the funding. The auto mechanic came back to town with the idea of a fund-raiser for the playground, championed by the kids in town. He got all the kids (to save their pennies), along with their moms and dads, and got everyone in town excited to participate in helping to fund and build a playground. He coaxed others into leadership roles. He convinced the construction division of the local National Guard to donate its time to put up the playground. He kept us all informed. He helped the kids understand how they were contributing with their pennies.

The architect arrived and codesigned the playground with the kids in an all-day, freewheeling design session. The pennies continued to pour in. A date was set, the Guard paraded down the main street, and the playground went up in two days with more than 150 volunteers doing the construction. The acceptance, ownership, and organization of fulfilling the goal completed the cycle of leadership.

The auto mechanic would not have been anyone's first choice as a leader if the town had put a playground on a master plan, funded it, put it out to bid, and awarded a construction company its bid. Popular wisdom would not have chosen someone who had zero experience in government, had even less experience in sports and recreation management, and was not very well known around town. The more likely leader would have been one of the town's administrative employees, someone with the requisite experience in handling building projects involving government funds. And the playground would have been simple and utilitarian. The auto mechanic was not the best dressed, not the strongest, not the biggest, and not the most experienced leader in town. He probably didn't grow up thinking about municipal playgrounds. But he was the one who saw the imbalance in the system; he was the one who articulated the goal; he was the individual we all associated with the goal; and he committed to being the leader, a leader with passion. He was not anyone's stereotypical leader; but he led. He had something he passionately wanted to do and couldn't do alone, so he engaged us all in a successful process. He had a purpose.

THE INNER GAME OF LEADERSHIP

We all have in our minds an image of a leader. We have biases and preferences based on stories, legends, and myths, as well as on movies, television shows, and life. At some point, we all seem to come to similar ideas that leaders should be the tallest, strongest, handsomest, and most intelligent. What we see in the media reinforces that. Then we see in the world what we've trained our mind to see. It is a biased and limited view of leadership. And notice, we don't necessarily include the idea of purpose-driven goals in our view of leadership. Most of us tie an image of a leader to our ultimate concept of a leader, and that image doesn't include an unseen intangible that is the core of leadership. We need to change our image of what a leader looks like.

A leader is someone who leads people based on a purposeful endeavor. Leaders come in all sorts of unexpected shapes, sizes, and genders, but what you can't see is a leader's inner purpose, commitment, and courage. The leader needs to communicate those things to us with words, deeds, and values. Too often our picture is based on the qualities that may not create the best leadership results.

There is no "look." You can't buy a suit of clothes that will turn you into a leader. There is no haircut or style that amps up your leadership effectiveness. There is no personality type that will make you a natural leader. Charm school might make you a better person but not a leader. Pure ambition won't work. Climbing the ladder might get you to a leadership role, but it won't necessarily make you a leader. Likewise, playing the organizational game—fitting in, pursuing all the training opportunities, finding a mentor, and doing everything right as you gain experience in leadership—may not be what it takes to make you a leader.

Our current image of a leader constructs an incomplete and potentially wrong picture of leadership. How many good leaders—leaders with a real sense of purpose—end up tossed aside because they do not match our image or picture of leadership? What would have happened in that small town if we had rejected the auto mechanic as our playground leader?

In the business world I've had the privilege to meet many great leaders. They have taught me more than I have taught them. I've

7

applied their lessons to my own leadership challenges. Frequently, I've come out on the better end; other times, I've not. The impact leaders have on their organizations is enormous. I have my leadership heroes. Frances Hesselbein led the turnaround of the Girl Scouts and was brought in by West Point Academy to revise its leadership curriculum. Alan Mulally led commercial aviation at Boeing before joining Ford Motor Company to turn it around. I watched William J. O'Brien, an architect of one of the original learning organizations, lead Hanover Insurance. These people led with vision and inspiration and a strong grasp of how to organize people to achieve that vision. They were guided by a strong sense of purpose, and they acted every day with purpose, conviction, ethics, and judgment. But they weren't the image of a typical leader. We see them today as impactful leaders, but each at times struggled with the fact that they didn't match the ideal.

These remarkable leaders, as well as other leaders I admire, had such a strong sense of personal purpose that they overcame the demands of external expectations. The research that Linkage conducted around leadership brought out this point: Leaders don't succumb to external expectations. They push past the external expectations with their belief in their purpose, their why. Our panel of experts said it perfectly with a tried-and-true saying: "The really effective leaders have the courage of their convictions."

Purposeful leaders are no different from the rest of us; there is no secret code to leadership. But something does spring from within. Out of the everyday, people who become leaders start asking themselves questions about what they see in the world, what they don't see and would like to, and what they perceive should change in the world. Purposeful leaders often ask themselves questions. Is there something that you are aching to accomplish? Do you have something burning inside you that needs to get done?

Do you have a problem that needs to get solved? Have you started working on it? What occurred or happened to you that is creating this burning desire? Who is with you? Are you clear about what needs to change to achieve this goal? Do you have a handle on organizing the effort? The people? The necessary technology? Do you have the financial resources, or do you need to secure them? If you have not gotten started, what's keeping you from starting? Are you missing a critical skill set? Are you part of an organization and need permission? Is your ache not part of your organization's strategy? Are you anxious about putting yourself out there? Is it too risky? Does it set you up for conflict with someone in your organization you don't want to deal with? Would pursuing this take you in a different direction than what your friends are taking? Do you think you might lose friends over this? Do you think you might fail? Are you not sure how to get started? Leaders see a gap in what is happening in their team, their function, their business, and bridging that gap becomes their purpose.

Leaders are not born; they are made from their experience. Experience drives a set of external skills and practices, but more importantly it drives an internal motivation or purpose. Leadership can be developed in all of us. Contrary to common wisdom, we are all leaders. If we set a goal that others follow, we are leading—even if we are terrible at it. It is sometimes hard to differentiate leaders from their goals. Even in those vast caverns of people called corporations, leadership can be very personal. But it is also social. Leadership is a team sport.

There's an old African proverb that "if you want to go fast, go alone. But if you want to go far, go together." In most endeavors where leadership adds value, you are trying to go far and attain a vision that is out in the future. Even building a playground in a small town can be a multi-year initiative and require more expertise and skill than is found in one person. Learning to lead a group of people to reach various goals of different scopes and scales is a lifelong journey. Leaders must be committed to their purpose, confident in their decisions, resolute in their drive, aware of their impact on others, and able to engage with different people with the complementary, requisite skills and knowledge to help reach the goal.

Leadership is important to long-term endeavors precisely because of the value it adds. Leaders organize engaged people in the pursuit of a goal or a vision they all find desirable. Reading a book will not make you a leader. This book will raise identify what you need to target to develop as a leader. It does not matter whether you are a CEO or an individual contributor: you can benefit by improving the inspirational nature of your vision; by connecting your vision to people who want to engage; by targeting the key areas in your organization that need to improve or change, by learning how to organize and structure people; and by finding and leveraging your own purpose.

There are people with no experience and no training who flourish as leaders. These are people who are inspired and who inspire, who care deeply about people, who put real thought into how things need to be different, and who know how to connect with others and how to connect others. They are courageous, self-aware, committed individuals dedicated to a purpose larger than themselves. They make lots of mistakes, but they speak powerfully to people and enlist others in their purpose. These unique people are many of the people Linkage studied and learned from in our curiosity to understand *purposeful leadership*. There are also individuals who are inspiring and own the leadership role in a company. As well intended as these individuals are, they are a riot of new ideas, poor communicators, socially immature, and constantly worrying about the wrong things or the expectations of others. They use resources to chase those distractions, creating disruption and disorganization. These leaders have plateaued.

My hope is that this book will help you think differently about your leadership. This book is based on six years of research analyzing more than 100,000 leaders from our database of leaders, an exhaustive review of the literature of leadership, interviews with some of the best leadership experts in the field, studying over 100 exemplars and multiple projects building leadership competency models. It is also derived from my own experience and ideas in watching and studying leaders—and in trying to be one myself. Since leadership is a community endeavor, we've also interviewed dozens of leaders to learn about their leadership journeys and extracted their leadership insights. It is safe to say that the people we have included in this book are all deeply curious students of leadership.

This book is organized into a series of chapters designed to reflect the way that purposeful leaders confront their challenges. The book is about the constant struggle to become a purposeful leader. Not every idea in this book will serve you well. But I have no doubt the basic principle or kernel of an idea, if you think about how to best apply it given who you are and your context, will be helpful. Even the simplest of leadership challenges can be quite the complex soup. In the end, you have to decide how you want to show up as a leader.

PURPOSEFUL LEADERSHIP

From our research, we have found that there are five critical commitments to a person's leadership:

1. Inspiring people toward a vision or a goal

2. Providing clarity on what needs to be changed or innovated to achieve that vision or goal

3. Engaging the skilled, knowledgeable stakeholders to make meaningful contributions to the vision or goal

4. Organizing and providing structure by putting people into teams, or groups that deliver success

5. Becoming a leader worth following by being committed, courageous, and self-aware

PRELIMINARY ASSESSMENT— WHERE DO YOU STAND?

Let's start with a measure of your purposeful leadership. I've provided an assessment below that will help you understand and target your acquisition of purposeful leadership. This assessment will map directly to the book and its commitments and practices.

You will work through 49 statements. Each is directly related to a key theme in the book. Place a check in the column you feel consistently represents your capability relative to the practice in the statement. If you have never had the chance to experience the practice stated, then you should check the box in the column labeled, "I haven't got a clue how to do this." The scale asks you your confidence in implementing the leadership behavior with three different sizes of community: small, medium, and large. Think about your company and your industry to define these sizes. In general, small would be fewer than 25 people. Medium would be between 25 and 500 people. Large would be anything above 500 people.

Item	Chapter	Item	I haven't got a clue how to do this.	I'm confident doing this with a small group of people.	I'm confident doing this with a medium-size group of people.	I'm confident doing this with a large group of people.
1.	3	My vision for the future gets people excited.				
2.	3	My plan for the organization leaves people knowing exactly what they need to do.				
3.	4	I keep talk about purpose and strategy interesting and straightforward.				
4.	3	I keep important messages short and sweet.				
5.	3	I keep the conversation moving in a positive direction.				
6.	4	I keep others' needs in mind when talking about my views and ideas.				
7.	4	I provide people and teams with a clear vision of future success and results.				
8.	4	I help people and teams overcome hurdles.				

Item	Chapter	Item	I haven't got a clue how to do this.	I'm confident doing this with a small group of people.	I'm confident doing this with a medium-size group of people.	I'm confident doing this with a large group of people.
9.	4	I make sure people know the value of the work they do.				
10.	5	My words and actions make other people feel comfortable speaking up.				
11.	5	I find out what makes people tick to better engage them.				
12.	5	I find common ground with others.				
13.	5	I make sure all people and teams feel included and valued.				
14.	5	I make sure all voices are heard.				
15.	5	I get insight from diverse perspectives across the organization.				
16.	5	I give people and teams appropriate challenges and stretch opportunities.				
17.	5	I make sure others are exposed to a wide variety of opportunities.				

Item	Chapter	Item	I haven't got a clue how to do this.	I'm confident doing this with a small group of people.	I'm confident doing this with a medium-size group of people.	I'm confident doing this with a large group of people.
18.	6	I make it clear that failure is not the end of the world but something to learn from.				
19.	6	I think outside the box to solve problems.				
20.	6	My ideas refresh and bolster people, teams, and the organization.				
21.	6	I keep up with and make sure others are aware of the latest industry trends and insights.				
22.	6	I engage a variety of stakeholders to test my ideas.				
23.	6	I figure out how change affects us and the work we do on all levels.				
24.	6	I consistently take a closer look at all levels of the organization to make sure we aren't missing opportunities.				

Item	Chapter	Item	I haven't got a clue how to do this.	I'm confident doing this with a small group of people.	I'm confident doing this with a medium-size group of people.	I'm confident doing this with a large group of people.
25.	6	I make sure everyone understands the case for change and how it addresses our organization's challenges and opportunities.				
26.	6	I make sure the path to change is clear of major obstacles.				
27.	6	I keep change initiatives running smoothly by making sure systems and processes are aligned at all levels.				
28.	8	I make sure people and teams are aware of how organizational processes support their objectives.				
29.	8	I make sure things get done by aligning the work across all levels of the organization.				
30.	8	I make sure the right people and teams are in the right roles.				

Item	Chapter	Item	I haven't got a clue how to do this.	I'm confident doing this with a small group of people.	I'm confident doing this with a medium-size group of people.	I'm confident doing this with a large group of people.
31.	8	I bring people and teams together by communicating shared goals.				
32.	8	I make sure individuals and teams have a say in decision making.				
33.	8	I inspire confidence and a sense of "can-do."				
34.	8	I adapt to the various obstacles in the organization's path at all levels.				
35.	9	I don't take my time to make confident and thoughtful decisions, even when the future is foggy.				
36.	9	I don't let problems fester—I take early action when I see something going wrong.				
37.	9	I adapt my style to work with the people and teams in front of me.				

Item	Chapter	Item	I haven't got a clue how to do this.	I'm confident doing this with a small group of people.	I'm confident doing this with a medium-size group of people.	I'm confident doing this with a large group of people.
38.	10	I always "walk my talk."				
39.	10	I acknowledge the limits of my own worldview to the people I'm working with.				
40.	10	I think about what's best for others, at every level of the organization, more than I think about what's best for me.				
41.	10	My decisions and actions keep the greater good of the organization at the forefront.				
42.	10	I keep my promises, no matter how specific or broad.				
43.	10	I keep true to myself and my values, no matter the situation.				
44.	10	I make the tough calls that need to be done.				

Item	Chapter	Item	I haven't got a clue how to do this.	I'm confident doing this with a small group of people.	I'm confident doing this with a medium-size group of people.	I'm confident doing this with a large group of people.
45.	10	I greet any organization challenge head-on.				
46.	10	I show people that I care.				
47.	10	I actually listen to individuals and teams, and I show that I understand their concerns.				
48.	10	I have a clear and transparent purpose to my leadership 49.				
49.	10	I bring out the best in people and teams.				

The results of this assessment reflect your opinion of who you currently are as a leader. Now that you have taken the assessment, you have a pretty good idea of where you need skill development and where you need experience to grow the scale of your leadership efforts. We can help you with the skills but not with the experience. I suggest you spend some time with the people you work with, asking them how well you do on some of these items.

There are multiple dimensions to consider as you grow:

- The cognitive, or intellectual, side of leadership that focuses on seeing or perceiving problems and opportunities and finding strategies and solutions

- The people, or experiential, side that focuses on working with people, teams, organizations, and even global cultures

- The personal side of things, what we refer to as becoming a leader: your philosophy or principles of leadership (sometimes called "your wisdom"), your standards or values, and your personal sense of purpose and how committed you are to it

You also need to consider whether you want to be a leader of large organizations, smaller divisions or teams, or individual contributors. In essence, purposeful leadership is about a way of being and of leading a community of people. Your principles will change over time as you experience the different types of leadership your organization or industry has to offer. Our idea of leadership, purposeful leadership, applies to all scopes and scales of leadership. Our research efforts covered global leaders, executives at large companies, entrepreneurs with their own companies, business leaders, geographic leaders, project leaders, team leaders, and thought leaders. However you choose to move forward in your leadership, it is my belief that you can become a better leader by practicing, seeking feedback, reflecting, getting uncomfortable with a new practice, and starting the cycle all over again.

Over the next few chapters we will talk about what makes leadership so difficult to acquire and develop (Chapter 1) and so difficult to learn (Chapter 2). We will then explore each of the five commitments of purposeful leadership, beginning with the importance of inspired goal setting (Chapter 3) and connecting to your purpose (Chapter 4). We will then help you master your purpose by putting your purpose to work in your leadership principles. As it always is with leadership, you will need to engage others in your vision, and we will help you to adopt an engagement mindset to make a positive difference in the lives of others working with you (Chapter 5). We then explore what is required to achieve your goal in the form of innovation or change. If you have set a great goal, then you will need to make substantial change to the current state of things to make it happen (Chapter 6). We will then take a quick look at a key dilemma that we all have as leaders: Whether to lead or to do (Chapter 7). This will lead us into how we structure people, process, and technology into a formula for success (Chapter 8). We will wrap up by looking at the power in leading purposefully and how you put it all together (Chapters 9 and 10).

We will follow three young leaders as examples of leaders in progress. *James*, *Priya*, and *Jane* will serve as exemplars of what each commitment of purposeful leadership looks like as it develops. In the last chapter, I'll fill you in on how each of their leadership journeys were fulfilled over time. Finally, each chapter will have a set of reflection questions for you to ask yourself or even engage with others as a means of elevating your leadership effectiveness.

We invite you to be purposeful in your leadership journey.

PART ONE

ASSESSING LEADERSHIP

A HUNGER FOR LEADERSHIP

Leadership is having a compelling vision, a comprehensive plan, relentless implementation, and talented people working together.

—*Alan Mulally, former President and CEO of Ford Motor Company*

DEFINING LEADERSHIP

In 1989, a professor in the business department at the University of Southern California published a book on leadership, *On Becoming a Leader*. The book created an industry of this new topic, leadership, as well as a new area of research. Warren Bennis had worked and taught at MIT in Boston, a center of research into organization development. Bennis himself had spent a lot of his energy trying to understand how teams work. And he jumped into the fray himself by becoming an administrator, and then the president of the

University of Cincinnati. After suffering a heart attack, he took a position at USC as a professor of management.

Bennis's key ideas were that leaders are: the author of their own story, that they learn from experience, and that they empower and organize others to make a vision come to life. Through his own insight and research, Bennis had come to the conclusion that a modern world of complexity, change, and information overload would require a new type of leadership: democratic or distributed leadership.

There are all sorts of leaders. Visions and goals, which are given life through people and energy, are what make leaders and leadership. Leadership is more than a title, a role, or a rank in an organization's hierarchy. If a group of people are trying to accomplish something, there will be a leader who has the respect and trust of the group. The leader will be the individual who is committed to the goal and pulls people together to achieve it. Although we can find hundreds of definitions of leadership, one definition really captures the essence: *Leadership is the engagement and mobilization of others to work in a structured way toward shared goals.*

Some leaders use inspiration and evocative communication to engage and mobilize people. Others use their own commitment and engagement to be an inspirational role model. Still other leaders work with people to create clarity in how things will be organized and structured. Many more leaders use all three combined. These last ones are what we call, "purposeful leaders." From years of observing and studying leaders in many industries, I know leadership is not just having skills; it's also valuing and committing yourself to the five basic responsibilities:

- The leader has a purpose and a vision that inspires others to join in its pursuit, something that will better the common good

- The leader engages every team member to contribute to their best abilities

- The leader drives new thinking and creative opportunities that creates competitive differentiation or an innovative way to the vision

- The leader helps to achieve results by creating structure: organizing people and aligning resources

- The leader transforms and grows themselves in their commitment, their courage, their self-awareness, and their ability to bring out the best in others through respect and involvement

In other words, to inspire, to engage, to innovate, to achieve, and to become. Any leader *must* have the dedication to all five of these commitments. But there is no one-size-fits-all leadership style or process.

OUR THREE LEADERS

Let's introduce our three leaders mentioned in the Introduction. *James* leads a group of approximately 70 people in the marketing function of a Fortune 100 company. He wants his company to succeed, and he wants to succeed. He is fabulous with the numbers and the financials of running his area. He hires great people and demands much from them. He is constantly focused on deliverables and outcomes. But something is missing. Even though he is a lifelong marketer, he doesn't have a real emotional connection to the product, the customer, or his team. He isn't committed to a purpose that is bigger than himself, that inspires him and others. His leadership feels onerous to others—mechanical and numbers-driven. When asked about it, he is frustrated by his people's reactions and shows significant irritation at being asked to be inspiring or visionary. He tends to be critical of people's work and often feels he is the only person who catches important details. He has a relatively high turnover rate in his department compared with the rest of the company, but he attributes that turnover to the luxurious salaries other companies are paying.

Priya leads a large division of about 225 people for a North American construction company. Her organization acquires clients, develops the project, builds the project, and warranties the project. Priya is a true engineering visionary. Her expectations of her people are vague—unarticulated and metaphorical—but demanding. Her department generates millions of dollars of profits when it is on target and millions of dollars of expense when wrong. She is constantly taking the risk on innovative new design-and-build projects. Also, when she notices employees in her department who display a strong construction sense, she mentors and coaches them. But she is highly disrespectful in the way she treats organizational systems and processes. Despite all this, she attracts a very dedicated group of employees who adore her and everything she does. They boldly imitate her reckless use of company systems.

Jane leads an enormous call center for her organization. Her 1,500-plus employees on three shifts find her to be the ultimate role model. She is professional yet warm, expert yet humble, kind yet firm. She gets to know all her employees personally and knows everyone's name. Beyond the daily routine of answering customer calls, though, most people describe her organization as a bit of a hot mess. Everything is done reactively and heroically. People love Jane, but not their jobs. Productivity drifts. Quality drifts. Frustration builds, a hero jumps in to save the day, and Jane holds a department ice cream social.

All three of these young leaders have been extensively trained in managerial and leadership skills and are considered by their organizations to be high potential. They have the skills, and all three value at least one or two of the commitments. Yet a purposeful leader must value and practice all the commitments, which are so important they bear repeating: to inspire, to engage, to innovate, to achieve, and to become. Yes, there are practices, even skills, that make up these commitments, but the purposeful leader strives every day to get better at the five commitments.

IDENTIFYING VALUED LEADERS

A cursory scan of business magazines, newspapers, and news programs on television would cause you to draw the conclusion that boards of directors of major companies are focused on finding, identifying, developing, and reaping the benefits of exceptional leaders. Investors seem to be betting heavily on software algorithms that can make leadership choices easy for them, hoping to take the variability, uncertainty, and risk out of their decisions. Such a management tool will help provide them with the right answer, the most predictable answer, the most controllable answer to the often-asked question: Who should lead? Would James, Priya, or Jane be tagged as an effective leader in these algorithms?

Estimates of spending on leadership development, succession planning, and talent management run into the billions of dollars globally ($300 billion). Companies build complex and complicated leadership development systems and programs to foster the growth of their Jameses, Priyas, and Janes. These systems and programs try to bring about the right mindsets and behaviors in leaders, so that they in turn can foster the culture and environment that will bring about business success.

These systems and programs are complicated. Many of these leadership development programs and systems rely heavily on principles of adult learning, which tend to focus on doing as learning. On-the-job development focused on assignments designed to enhance, amplify, and extend an individual's leadership capabilities is vitally important to most organizations' plans around building leaders. Each assignment is chosen to enhance the ability of potential leaders to understand and manage each function in the organization in the belief that someday they will be able to meld it all together. Less frequently, but still in many organizations, there are also activities designed to broaden a leader's understanding of customers, the industry, the economy, global trends, ethics, and the future. The pieces and parts of these systems include training programs to foster skills. These skills focus on such things as strategy development, financial acumen, operations management, change management, innovation, communication skills, and decision making as well as emotional intelligence, influencing, and coaching.

Once we identify the leaders of the future, we often put them through a leadership development program. James, Priya, and Jane have been through multiple weeks of leadership training with varying degrees of effectiveness.

James, Priya, and Jane will need to build the capability of melding all the functions that make up an organization: the social or cultural system or systems, the political systems, the business systems, the regulatory or legal systems, the territorial or geographic systems, the technology systems, the shareholder or ownership structure, and the economic and competitive systems—just to name a few.

DEVELOPING AND GROOMING LEADERS

Companies also invest in succession planning as a way to influence who the next leader will be. Processes exist that identify, evaluate, and cultivate high-potential individuals as they transition through the value stream of the business and the various functions of the company. These succession planning systems are often supported by multiple assessments (both objective and subjective), multiple levels of review and study, and development plans to ensure the growth of the individual and ensure his or her readiness to take on more responsibility. Having the requisite capabilities to govern large complex organizations is the ultimate leadership capability that most of these processes are trying to cultivate. All three of our exemplars—James, Priya, and Jane—have been identified as potential successors to their executive leaders. As they grow and become responsible for more of their whole organizations, the complexities and the nuances of leadership will increase.

It is a big responsibility for an individual to create the right goals or vision, find talented and engaged people, and develop and implement a plan, all while fostering the future talent of the organization. Of course, the very high failure rate of leaders at large organizations should tell us a lot about how successfully these succession planning processes actually perform. Executive leaders face immense difficulty in choosing whom to invest in for the future.

Outwardly, the criteria seem to be, first, who will be best to lead the business. Second, who will be best to lead the organization. Third, who will be best to create the future. We also know that human decision making is rife with bias. At Linkage, we find that building these succession systems to be as objective and fair as possible requires a great deal of thought around some demanding, difficult, and complex processes. When a diverse slate of candidates goes into a succession planning meeting and tall, white males are the only high potentials that come out as a result, something has gone wrong. Something went powerfully wrong. Similarly, when the slate of leaders is identified and all the high-potential individuals are people that no one wants to actually work for or follow, something went wrong. The same can be said of hiring systems: The identification of leaders to hire from outside an organization can be daunting and statistically has a low success rate. Virtually 60 percent of outside hires into leadership positions are, at some level, unsuccessful: The outside hires fail to achieve all the expectations that were laid out. It is safe to say that when we identify leaders, we often look at the wrong things or attribute the wrong characteristics to our definition and criteria.

The literature surrounding leadership is filled with all sorts of estimations, prognostications, and educated guesses about what will make a great leader. For businesses, the dominant criteria, usually spoken and transparent, are revenue growth and profit. These criteria often override other considerations. While all leaders are human beings and flawed, based on our research and data, leaders are first and foremost leaders of organizations of people. People in organizations create business results. As William J. O'Brien, the CEO of Hanover Insurance, learning organization proponent, and one of my early role models, said, "Human capital drives financial capital." Therefore, leaders must be good for people and for the culture of the organization. It is sometimes easy for executives to conflate the aroma of revenue and profit with what is perceived as ambition, toughness, and determination that can go overboard into the stench of destruction. It is all too easy to say that business skills are hard skills and leadership skills are soft skills, and as a result to judge hard skills as much more important than soft skills. Or worse, judge one as optional relative to the other. The road that James, Priya, and Jane are traveling is fraught with all sorts of business, organizational, and leadership challenges. Linkage's own research found that only one in five American workers believes his or her organization is led by a "purposeful leader."

PURPOSEFUL LEADERSHIP INDEX

As a leadership development firm, Linkage has worked directly with more than 1 million leaders over the past 30 years. During that time, we have directly assessed approximately 106,000 leaders, looking at their perceptions of themselves, as well as their behaviors, attitudes, and performance through the lens of their peers, bosses, and direct reports. Each of these leaders has on average, 10 raters. In all, this is more than a million data points.

Given the challenge that most leadership models and theories are based primarily on case studies, biographies, anecdotes, and psychological research, we sought to build a leadership framework based both on evidence and examination of the assessment data we have, layered with academic and client perspectives, and on review of third-party research.

Our research team conducted a meta-analysis of the multiple data points to understand what distinguishes great leaders from their less effective peers. To normalize for factors such as luck, macroeconomic environment, industry, or sector, we defined "great" as being rated in the top 10 percent each by peers, subordinates, and supervisors. What we discovered was that the best leaders are, above all else, purposeful. They are driven by their purpose and how they do things is on purpose.

Juxtaposed against accidental leaders (who may tend to be careless, thoughtless, purposeless, even reckless), purposeful leaders are "-ful": thoughtful, careful (though not necessarily cautious), hopeful. Purpose is the effective leader's tool.

In the first half of 2017, Linkage undertook a national survey of the working population in the United States to assess the impact that purposeful leadership has on employee attitudes and organizational performance. More than 1,000 respondents assessed their organization's leadership across a range of purposeful leadership behaviors, attitudinal outcomes, and organizational performance metrics. The results, quantified in the Linkage Purpose Index, validate the data upon which the Linkage Purposeful Leadership model is based.

The Linkage Purpose Index explores the effect of purposeful leadership on four essential business indicators: financial performance, competitive differentiation, employee engagement, and employee-driven net promoter score.

The Linkage Purpose Index survey first identified working respondents and asked survey participants to score their leaders on a range of behaviors that are most predictive of purposeful leadership. A few examples of the behaviors are:

- Distills ideas into focused messages that inspire support or actions from others

- Earns stakeholder commitment by looking for and bringing out people's potential

- Articulates a compelling future for the organization that guides clear action and behavior

- Communicates viewpoints in a way that positively influences the dialogue

- Fosters collaboration among people or teams by aligning goals and expectations, and monitoring teamwork

- Makes people feel proud and part of something bigger than themselves

- Acts and speaks with consistency, as if aligned to a personal sense of purpose

- Acts and makes decisions in alignment with organizational purpose and direction

This behavioral profile identified the top quartile of leaders (as determined by the aggregate scores given by respondents) as purposeful leaders. It's a lot to process, but it really boils down a few basics:

- Be good for the people in your organization

- Be a positive influence on the culture of your organization

- Set great goals that elevate your business results and competitiveness

YOU HAVE THE DATA. NOW ACT ON IT

According to the 2017 Gallup *State of the American Workplace* report, only 21 percent of employees "strongly agree that their performance is managed in a way that motivates them to outstanding work." That metric alone proves that there's a lot of room for leaders to grow, but when it comes to specifics on what employees actually want from their leaders, hard data isn't easy to come by. There are hundreds of blog posts about what makes a good leader, but not much of that comes from the mouths of those who actually follow.

In their book, *Strengths Based Leadership* (2009), Tom Rath and Barry Conchie analyzed a Gallup study that surveyed more than 10,000 employees in "follower" roles from 2005 to 2008. From this study, four focus areas that followers look for in their leaders emerged: They want leaders who show *compassion* and can be *trust*ed and who can provide *stability* and *hope*. While these are somewhat broad and nebulous concepts, they lay the foundation for how a leader should treat employees.

A more recent study from Dale Carnegie Training offers a few more concrete skills that employees want their leaders to practice. In a global online survey of more than 3,300 full-time employees, there were four leadership characteristics most frequently cited by participants as motivating them to do their best work. People want their leaders to give them sincere appreciation, admit when they are wrong (fostering a sense of psychological safety), truly listen to and respect employees' opinions, and be both externally reliable (dependable) and internally reliable (consistent in words and actions). These findings are mirrored in the *State of the American Workplace* study cited earlier. Employees' most frequent complaints about their supervisors are (1) unclear expectations, (2) ineffective or infrequent feedback, and (3) accountability concerns.

Linkage's Purposeful Leader Assessment is a 360-degree feedback instrument with an added element of several research questions. We ask three questions of the raters but not the participant leaders themselves:

- Is this leader good for people?

- Is this leader good for the culture?

- Is this leader good for the business?

The results are startling. Less than 20 percent of leaders scored either a four or a five on even one of these three questions (based on a five-point scale). Less than one in five leaders is good for people, good for the culture, or good for the business. When we calculate the percentage of leaders who are good for all three, we get only 9 percent. For all the money and time we spend developing leaders, we should be getting better results.

As Thomas Kolditz, who wrote the Foreword for this book, has written, "Never let anyone say that leadership gains are intangible or impossible to measure." What is more important is believing the statistics you have and acting on them.

Our way of looking at leaders and leadership has probably served us well for thousands of years. It has also created many counterproductive outcomes and excluded a vast majority of the planet from potentially being included in this endeavor called leadership. Our gut reactions can be quite sophisticated at picking whom to lead, but there are also powerful forces that make our judgments about leaders unreliable. We should be able to do better than one in five leaders being effective.

As an industry, leadership development has concentrated on skills and competencies as the method of developing a leader. Yet leadership is, as Bennis put it, "self-invention." People are what make up leadership. People want leaders who inspire them and give them both hope and meaning. People want leaders who will engage them and let them contribute their skills, their talents, and their ideas. People want something to change. They want to see new ways of doing things or new ideas permeate the system. They understand that to achieve a goal, something about the way things are being done needs to be different. People want to be organized. They want clarity on how to work together. This is the essence of "purposeful leadership": fulfill the expectations of the people who work with you and around you. Great goals, whether they are business goals or organizational goals or civic goals, happen as a result of leadership.

You are probably a leader who wants to improve your leadership and your outcomes. If so, and if you really want to make a change, you must be ready to ask, answer, and change your thinking around some difficult questions.

LEADERSHIP PROBE

- What are your leadership challenges? These are challenges within you, not external challenges. Are you good for the people around you? Are you a positive influence on your organization's culture? Are you adding value to the business itself?

  - Do people who work for you become better assets for your organization as a result of your direct intervention?

  - Does the culture of the organization you lead become more inclusive, efficient, and stable over time?

  - Does the organization you lead contribute business value to the mission of your organization?

- How might you go about getting honest and valuable feedback on your leadership? Whom would you ask? What data would you dig up? Whom might you enlist to help you interpret the data and the feedback?

- Have you perhaps gotten good enough just to get by? How would you know? How would you know that you have lots more potential but haven't done the work to manifest it? Lots of us take up a hobby or a sport, and we get "good enough" pretty quickly, but we stop investing the energy and time we need to really excel.

- What do you think makes a great leader for your organization? What actions are good for people? Are good for the culture? Are good for the business?

- Do you deeply understand the contributions that each of your employees is capable of making?

- How would you measure leadership in your organization to produce better outcomes?

THE MYSTERY
OF LEADERSHIP

Leadership is a matter of how to be—not how to do it.
—Frances Hesselbein, President and CEO,
Frances Hesselbein Leadership Institute

BECOMING: BEYOND MYSTERY
TO MASTERY

In *The Hero with a Thousand Faces,* Joseph Campbell, a comparative mythologist and philosopher, developed a grounded theory of the hero's journey. It became the character outline for Luke Skywalker in *Star Wars.* When the original *Star Wars* opens, Luke is a young, frustrated dreamer living with his family on a virtually uninhabited planet. A chance encounter with a droid leads him to go find a mystical warrior supposedly living nearby. Luke, sensing the excitement, wants to follow the droids and the warrior on an adventure, if his family approves. But the situation is drastically altered when he returns home and finds his family murdered. It is obvious that he and the droids are also targets. The warrior is wise and promises to train young Luke in the ways of the Jedi. Along the way, there are missteps, princesses in distress, mistakes, awkward situations, failures, romance, villains, death and losses, and small and large successes, and through each new experience the young Jedi advances in wisdom, strength, courage, and even compassion. The test comes when he must rely on all his new instincts to face the enemy who could destroy his universe. Luke is not born a great warrior. He must be trained. As *Star Wars* closes, he is trained enough to be dangerous. He knows nothing of the Jedi, and yet he becomes the symbol and hope for the future.

The story is simple enough while also complex and mystifying. What took a farmer all the way to *symbolic warrior*? He's not anything we would picture in terms of a warrior.

This is also true of the warrior who trains him. Both are slight, with little obvious muscle. Yet they win light saber battles with their hearts and their heads. This was a key idea as the writers worked from Joseph Campbell's archetype to shape Luke, the unlikely warrior.

This journey of the hero in many ways parallels the becoming of a leader. We find our warrior inside us. We find our leadership inside us.

We make leadership public in how and where we choose to stand, how and what we say, what we choose to reveal or conceal, what we focus on and what we don't, how we show emotion, and in what we physically do. As people looking at leaders, we must look for clues. We cannot see inside a leader's heart or mind. We must deduce leadership from what we physically see. We can remove some of the mystery of leadership, but there is always a piece that we cannot know for sure.

The mystery of leadership lies in the puzzle pieces of the goal, the social dynamic, the collective of leaders, and the internal journeys. As individuals, we each put the puzzle pieces together in slightly different ways, just as Winston Churchill put them together one way, Mahatma Gandhi another, Nelson Mandela yet a different way, and Justice Ruth Bader Ginsburg in her way. All four are from roughly the same era, dealing in many ways with similar yet somewhat different challenging world circumstances. None of these individuals invites much comparison with the others, and yet they all symbolize leadership.

Leadership is also not necessarily for the famous.

Leadership exists in landscaping teams, quick-service restaurants, retail stores, elementary schools, facilities management crews, hospital wards and specialty units, governmental entities at all levels, and musical ensembles. Regardless of the type of entity, there are individuals out front setting a goal, engaging others to contribute to the goal, finding and targeting an area where one new thing will make the goal possible, and organizing people to bring it all to fruition.

As they pursue this, they are wondering: *Who am I as a leader? Do I have what it takes? Do I have the wisdom? The conviction? The resilience? Am I willing to shoulder the burden of what it is going to really take? Can I go from an isolated leader who feels lost trying to make something happen to a connected, fulfilled, open human being who is leading others to a satisfying goal?*

The mystery of leadership also lies in the very concept of leadership itself. What is it? Our research process took us through a great many different definitions and theoretical explanations. We went through every argument and theory that has been posited, and we tried to build on the shoulders of many great researchers and writers. Simply, leadership is the engagement and mobilization of people in realizing some shared goal or opportunity. It may exist in an individual, but it also exists among all the individuals involved in an endeavor. We as academics, theorists, and organizational specialists have turned leadership into a messy, complex, misunderstood enigma.

What Is Leadership?

If you are feeling confused by this stretched concept of leadership, what it is and what it is not, you are not alone. What often makes this tricky is our confounding of the concept of leadership with management, with power roles in organizations, and with certain skills or traits that leaders have and don't have. The leader used to be the "one in charge." But that is too simple.

Roughly and loosely, a leader is the one who has an organizing influence over a group to accomplish or achieve a specific shared goal, a goal that has a common good attached to it. Still, in many companies or organizations, this is not so simple. There are different types of leaders and different aggregations of leaders. While our young Luke is a dreamy-eyed young man seeking adventure and romance in the world, he quickly becomes engaged in a bigger, more dramatic shared goal—the defeat of the Empire and the Emperor. The world as Luke and his friends know it is in danger, and it threatens them all. Luke is now one of many leaders and sits within one of many different groups of leaders; he is part of leadership.

The concept of leader and leadership is not that difficult. In any sport, the leader is the standard-bearer, the one out front, the pace-setter. Outside of sports, the leader is the goal-setter, the tempo-setter, the individual or individuals who are in command, or just the person out front and visible to the rest of the world as the "one who is responsible." Nelson Mandela believed that sometimes leaders are out front, but mostly they are leading from the back, letting their talented peers be the ones out front. The leader is the individual who creates, inherits, or owns the goal to create a positive difference in some opportunity or situation.

Complex Problems

These are simplistic ways of making leadership mysterious. The essence of leadership is about people. It's about creating a collection of people who want to accomplish something. A very real trap that leaders fall into is focusing on the technical problems and not the people problems. We want a better machine, a better software product, or a better process, and we put all our mental energy into the design and development of that thing. But our job as leader is to gather, organize, energize, and inspire talented people to come together and solve the problem. Some leaders get so focused on the problem they forget they have people working with them. Consider the thought experiment where you put someone into a leadership role who has no idea what the organization does. That would be disastrous, would it not? In the same way, think of the person who is put into a leadership role who does not know how an organization of people works. We do this all the time, don't we? We put technical experts in organizational leadership roles and are surprised when they focus on the problem and not the people. *This is a direct result of our failure to understand the true nature of leadership.*

Leaders often succeed through luck. For example, if an organization establishes a certain problem or issue needs to be resolved, they put a leader with a team and challenge them to solve the problem. While the group is a cognitively diverse group of people, they often see themselves as the experts assembled to solve the problem. Each team member holds different knowledge and has different experience. Each is usually incentivized to solve the issue. In groups, there are interpersonal dynamics that make it hard for everyone to contribute. When one individual—and a great majority of the time it's the leader—comes up with an answer, the team's work is done. In other words, in most teams it is the work of the lone genius that creates success. No one has to work together. No one has to build on anyone else's ideas. No one has to collaborate. In many cases, the group just has to please the boss with whatever answer the boss thinks is correct. It may not be the best answer, or a great answer, but it is an answer that suffices.

Since this can work a vast majority of the time, it becomes our belief of leadership. Unfortunately, this only works until the challenge becomes too great, and the leader doesn't have a different understanding of how to lead a group purposefully. The enterprise starts to unravel. Leadership that understands every problem as a simple problem is not prepared to deal with the messy, complex problems that really determine the future of an organization.

Purposeful leadership is the capability to formulate a goal or a vision that is inspiring to many people. It is then collecting together the talent and skill that will meaningfully contribute to that goal. But this group, the group working with the purposeful leader, doesn't depend on the lone genius to find an answer. Instead, it is organized and structured to think together, ideate together, innovate together, and build wisdom together to create an answer that one lone genius could never think of alone. The collective ability of the team outperforms the ability of any one person. All the team members are inspired by the goal, engaged with each other and the goal, and innovate to achieve the goal through the organization and structure provided by their leadership. This is why leadership is so mysterious: By not truly understanding the generative nature of leadership, we create all sorts of issues and traps for ourselves, for our leaders, and for our organizations.

In addition, what we really don't understand fully, what is mysterious to us, is the very nature of leadership problems. Leadership problems are not linear, simple problems. They are messy, complex, sticky problems with both seen and unseen variables. Linear problems are easy to solve. Messy, complex, sticky problems keep us actively engaged in either finding easy solutions that eventually will be shown not to work or reducing the messiness and complexity of the problem to a simple story that has an easy answer and long-term negative impacts. Unfortunately, over time both alternatives will lead to an even stickier, messier, and more complex problems.

Leaders Resolve Dilemmas

Leaders don't have problems to solve; they live in the land of dilemmas. It is this distinction between a dilemma and a problem that creates the mystery at the heart of leadership. Leadership is making choices between two or more, sometimes positive, alternatives where there is no simple answer. Simply put, does a leader with growing pains and cash that needs to be invested spend that cash on a marketing campaign, an upgrade to an enterprise software system, a new generation of talent that needs to be hired, or maybe a little in all three? Leaders deal with all sorts of dilemmas every day.

The Short Term Versus the Long Term

The first dilemma or trap that many leaders fall prey to is the short-term versus long-term strategy. For example, as a leader I have as a responsibility the care and maintenance of a facility. Buildings require lots of upkeep and maintenance. Well, I can do the maintenance, and I can put aside funds for future maintenance needs, but that eats into my short-term need to be profitable quarterly and annually. By deferring the maintenance, I can improve my bottom line, and my successor can deal with maintenance issues if they become problematic. I can also delay training classes or eliminate leadership development. I can undercapitalize the business as a whole and reap the benefits today.

As a leader I can take shortcuts as a means of boosting my profitability. I can ignore the signs of change in my markets and just ride it out with my current products and services. Or I can choose to make all my employees exempt, as opposed to nonexempt, and avoid paying and managing overtime. I can expect my leaders to lead, to manage, and to carry a full-time individual contributor role. I can reduce some difficult and demanding choices to overly simplistic answers that will provide immediate benefit.

Leadership Is Ethics

A leader faces a second dilemma when choosing to take the easy road ethically. Here are just a few instances where ethical lapses are all too easy:

- Turning down a warranty claim because it was filed one day after the warranty expired.

- Refusing to repair a badly installed window that is leaking in the house that your company built and sold.

- Going back on a promise you made to a high-performing employee by not paying his bonus because it will hurt the bottom line.

- Ignoring the toxic leader working for you because she is delivering the highest amount of profit in the business.

- Treating a direct report of yours differently because that report is your superior's favorite. Does he get preferential treatment? Do his lapses get dealt with equitably compared with how other employees are treated?

- Allowing your favorite employee to dress a lesser standard than everyone else.

- Listening to one group of people more than others. Heeding one group over another.

- Being hypervigilant in paying attention to shareholders compared with customers or employees.

- Being highly critical of a vendor's performance simply to find a way to lower the vendor's invoice.

- Being deliberately vague and ambiguous with an employee to guarantee that she won't be successful.

A leader's ethics and character are highly visible to those around them. The choices that a leader makes create the culture of the organization and will determine the respect that leader garners. There is real mystery here. Even though it's absolutely clear that leaders should demonstrate professional, ethical behavior around their distinct set of responsibilities, it's not always clear how leaders should go about resolving these dilemmas given the pressures of profit-and-loss statements and quarterly earnings reports.

No one really prepares us for the maturity, wisdom, and courage sometimes required of us.

No one really thinks that immediately repairing a hole in the parking lot should take courage or wisdom. Putting it off can save $1,000. Putting off many of these decisions to take action can save potentially a hundred thousand dollars for an organization. That's budget magic—just defer some decisions. What takes wisdom, maturity, and courage is not deferring these types of decisions, whether it's fixing a pothole or finding ways to rethink and rebalance the organization's pricing models, expenses, and competitive intelligence. Healthy, viable business decisions manage dilemmas successfully. No one will see a leader as wise, mature, and courageous when a pedestrian breaks an ankle after stepping into the hole in the parking lot (just ask an old insurance underwriter like me). And no one will continue to fully trust that leader either. When we resolve the dilemma in favor of one overwhelming and unbalanced consideration and negative consequences arise from it, the aroma around our leadership brand begins to stink . . . then reek.

The Pressure for Approval

A third dilemma arises when we ponder the dramatic rise in the importance of the shareholder's voice in our organizations. Shareholders buy into our organizations in different ways, but largely it is to see the value of their investment grow over time with the rise of the stock price. Even in not-for-profit organizations or contributors give to see an accelerated change in some issue or concern through the organization's contribution to the issue. These various shareholders often have a greater voice in the organization's major decisions, either in who gets elected to the board of directors or by becoming a member of the board themselves. Essentially, shareholders are only concerned with the profitability or the outcomes of their investment.

Shareholders want the most return for the least amount of input. They want the value of the company to increase as much as possible for their investment. When that does not happen, they often sell their shares and invest elsewhere. Leaders of the organization constantly feel the pressure to increase the company's performance as quickly as possible to maintain the investments.

Uncertainty and volatility create even bigger problems for leaders making big, strategic decisions. Paying for something today that may not have an effective return for a long time, maybe decades or perhaps not at all, increases shareholder concerns. The shareholder is interested in this quarter and this year, while the leader should be interested in both this quarter and the future. Succumbing to one priority over another may hurt the leader's trustworthiness and value. Adding to the pressure, boards and shareholders sometimes create compensation packages and golden parachutes that align the leader's self-interest with the self-interest of the board and shareholders to maximize the value of their investment in the shortest time possible. When this happens, the leader's choices fail to live up to his or her other long-term duties and responsibilities. When we make leaders completely accountable to the present, we endanger the future to which they have significant obligations. This can be a serious trap for leaders. Ultimately, when leaders succumb to these types of pressures and get into other issues that are a direct result of ignoring the future, we often talk of the leaders' lack of skills or the decline of their character.

Leaders need to think about these dilemmas as *tensions.* Instead of treating them as problems on a never-ending to-do list, they need to understand and manage dilemmas as things that will never go away; the dilemmas may disappear or hide from view, but that is part of the deceptiveness of dilemmas. Every business has a dozen or so dilemmas that come and go over time, sometimes resolving themselves successfully with no action on the part of leaders or leadership. But each of those dilemmas is still there and still operating, and when it suddenly reemerges and reveals its uglier side, we are perplexed.

THE PERSONAL BACKLASH: CAN WE TRUST OUR LEADERS?

The many traps that can ensnare leaders also cause a more insidious problem: They can destroy trust. According to global PR giant Edelman in its annual Trust Barometer—an exhaustive research study that has been conducted for the past 18 years—trust in the institution of leadership is at an all-time low. The 2018 survey results show an unchanged distrust in institutions, businesses, and governments. The data suggests that we perceive leaders as self-interested and greedy with low ethical standards. In other words, leaders are resolving the dilemmas in a one-sided and unbalanced way.

By not balancing the dilemma, leaders eventually are seen as untrustworthy. When people believe their leaders are untrustworthy, they retire, leave, or hide in their cubes. They disengage. And disengaged people are not innovative or creative. They hunker down and make friends with the status quo. The neuroscience of disengagement is rock solid: People stop performing at all but the most basic survival level. As of 2018, Gallup reports that only 18 percent of the global workforce is actively engaged. This is a serious indictment of leadership effectiveness.

As Frances Hesselbein, quoted at the start of the chapter, said, "Dispirited, unmotivated, unappreciated workers cannot compete in a highly competitive world." In the very act of leaders advancing their own interests or single-mindedly advancing only the shareholders' interests (with which theirs are aligned), the leaders create cynicism. Further, by leaving in place leaders who struggle with wisdom, conviction, purpose, courage, and character, boards and executives confuse all stakeholders about what leadership really is. In our minds, it reduces the standard of leadership. It destroys or confuses our mental models of leadership. We come to believe that leadership is something other than what we know in our hearts it is. Then, when someone rises above the fray and truly leads, we may not attribute what they do to leadership itself.

FINDING THE WHY: SWEET SYMPHONY

Standing at the front of a group of people is symbolic of the impact that we, as leaders, have on others. It is also symbolic of how effective leadership can help create a collective effort where everyone is aligned, engaged, and moving forward in the same direction. Standing at the podium in front of an orchestra is also symbolic of leadership. A conductor leading a finely tuned orchestra playing in perfect unison is a symbol that many researchers have used to describe leadership.

At Linkage's annual Global Institute of Leadership Development, which draws close to 500 leaders annually, one of our faculty members is a conductor who uses his skills to describe the systemic issues of leading a large organization. He always concludes by explaining that leading an orchestra is a metaphor for the meaning of leadership. At the same time he brings the message of classical music to the masses. By sharing his podium experience with corporate types who crave insights about leadership, he broadens their understanding and appreciation of his first love, music. He shares his baton. He shares his passion.

This metaphor provides a shared insight and experience of leadership to a group of people. This is the essence of purposeful leadership. The purposeful leader embodies wisdom, conviction, responsibility, commitment, openness, and belief in others and their capabilities.

The essence of purposeful leadership is finding the "why" within yourself and then enlarging your podium to include other leaders who have similar "whys" or who are inspired enough to adapt your why. The purposeful leader uses this collective energy to organize and stimulate efforts to achieve the why. But leadership starts with self-understanding, with understanding our purpose, our gifts, our own knowledge, and our experience base. It starts with an inner journey.

As leaders, we move around to different teams, functions, divisions, and businesses, each of which has different scale, scope, value contribution, and expertise. When we accept leadership of these different groups, the members of the groups instantly form expectations of us as their leader. (*Caution:* They don't instantly accept us as their leader.)

From there, our actions as the leader create a social dynamic that accelerates and augments the performance and behavior of that group. We walk around, assess, investigate, question, challenge, and get clear about what is and what could be. As leaders, we aren't outside the process, observing from a distance or receiving secondhand reports; we are acting out the process. It is both subjective and objective. We bring who we are, what we've experienced, and what we have learned, know, and believe to this process. We also bring our emotions, our ambitions, and our conviction that we are the right one to lead. Finally, we bring our sense of what we want to happen: our "why" we want to lead. We believe in what we are doing, following our instincts and experience, being authentic to who we are and open to the outcomes.

Leadership doesn't start with a need to be in a certain role or have a certain title. It starts with bringing our full self to an opportunity or a problem. It continues with our capability to articulate that opportunity or problem in a way that inspires and engages others (and enlarges the podium). It is accelerated by our ability to think through and target the right innovations that move an opportunity or problem to a different level. It is focused by our skills in organizing people to achieve that opportunity or problem. It is then enhanced and accelerated by our sense of self: our character and presence, our wisdom and courage, our commitment and focus.

BECOMING A LEADER

Every tradition has its mythology, its legend, its narrative about the inner journey. That journey carries the challenge, the excitement, the fear of the unknown, the sheer terror of failing, the uncertainty of the reward, the loneliness, the companionship, the outer struggle, and the inner belief in oneself. All of this is *becoming*.

For a leader, the becoming is usually a path that involves hiring and firing people, evaluating subordinates, having difficult conversations, leading teams, leading projects, turning a business around, starting up a new function or business, working with a special group of peers on some initiative, dealing with challenging economics or customers, delivering bad news or receiving bad news, leading people around celebrations or traditions, and watching peers come and go as they retire or move on.

How we show up as we move through all these events builds our identity and reputation as a leader. We move through these events, we find or receive feedback, we increase our self-awareness, our conviction to do better increases, and we grow with each challenge. We also grow in self-efficacy that we are on the right inner path to being a leader. Each day we grow more certain of why we choose to be a leader.

Each day, we can demonstrate this to others a little better. Leadership is not a collection of competencies and skills. It is a set of commitments we make to ourselves and others to *become* the best leader we can be. In the next few chapters we will explore these commitments and show you how they will make you a better leader.

CONTEXT AND CHALLENGES PROBE

- As you look back on the leaders you have trusted and respected the most and the least, what are some lessons you learned watching them navigate various dilemmas?

- Make a list of the characteristics and skills that make a leader.

- As you look at various leaders in your present, what makes them leaders to your way of thinking? What boxes do they tick off on your list?

- Make a list of dilemmas confronting you as a leader.

- For each dilemma, what are the consequences of resolving the dilemma one way or the other?

- How would a wise, mature, courageous leader manage each

of these dilemmas? What pressures and demands would you face that could unravel that leadership path? How do you know that you might be succumbing to the pressures?

- As you look at other leaders in your organization, do you see them differently given these insights?

- Are you susceptible to reducing messy stories to simple problems and simple solutions?

- Do you want to belong more than you want to do the right thing?

- Do you study the ethics of leadership?

PART TWO

INSPIRE

3

FINDING AND
FRAMING THE GOAL

We have enough people who tell it like it is. Now we could use a few
people who tell it like it could be.

—Robert Orben, author and comedian

COMMITMENT: INSPIRE
*Provide hope and inspiration for the future
and direct energy toward a bold vision.*

In our research into leadership, we analyzed the data to figure out
which of our five commitments is most strongly associated with
highly effective leaders. And while all five are highly correlated with
effectiveness, inspiration is the most highly correlated.

How many times have we heard a story about an academic thesis written by a graduate or undergraduate student that becomes a

reality? In 1989, Wendy Kopp wrote such a sociology thesis about people choosing to make a difference in the world rather than making money. Her generation, she was convinced, was about purpose and meaning. The opportunity she navigated to make a difference was in education; she saw geography as a limiting force in equality. She believed in the power of her generation as future leaders, and she founded Teach for America, a nonprofit dedicated to providing an excellent education to children who live in poverty in the United States. Every year, more than 8,000 young men and women go through a rigorous selection program to qualify for a two-year assignment in one of 51 regions in the United States. For more than 20 years, Wendy Kopp's vision has inspired and energized thousands of young men and women to put aside their lives and work for the benefit of others and the future opportunities they might achieve. By energizing young leaders to not just teach, but also lead social change, Wendy Kopp changed the trajectory of thousands of lives across America. She framed a goal and a vision, and then raised the capital, gathered the talent to make it happen, and innovated new teaching methods and approaches to social change. She organized the management team, the board of directors, a regional approach, and an international network of similar approaches. A simple undergraduate thesis, in inspiring hands, changed the world for more than three million children and 33,000 teachers.

Like most leaders, Kopp is a product of her time and context: the different scenarios playing out in the world. Trends and possibilities that were undiscussable, unknowable, or perceived by only a few. Multiple dilemmas, not one. Kopp approached these myriad dilemmas by creating a call to action to resolve them. She set a "vision for what could be." She also knew she could not achieve the vision alone. She understood that to achieve her vision she needed the engagement and talents of many others.

Many leaders have done something similar with a vast array of challenges that were manifest in their context. Purposeful leaders provide hope and inspiration for the future and direct energy toward a bold vision. This is the first commitment of purposeful leadership: *to inspire*. The value a leader brings to a group is the ability to inspire that group to a vision. A goal or a vision is almost never one's greatest fear but rather a leader's (or group of leaders') greatest hope about what the leader and the group can bring about together. Messages of hope are contagious and uplifting, and they give people a reason to believe in the future. Wendy Kopp didn't look at the geographic discrepancies in education funding and quality and despair; instead, she saw a path to provide hope and opportunity. Was this done in one giant leap? Of course not. She did many things as an undergraduate besides write a thesis on the subject that prepared her for what became her mission, a mission that inspired others to give as much of themselves. Did she instantaneously articulate a perfect vision her first time out? Of course she didn't. She sharpened her message in multiple conferences and a variety of colloquiums before writing her thesis. She engaged with her advising professor and mentor in hours of conversation. After graduating, she honed her message in recruiting talent to her mission and in raising capital for the enterprise. Kopp's was an endless process of tuning, refining, editing, and shaping.

We can inspire others in many ways: being a role model, showing courage in a situation that others find difficult, or being vulnerable in front of others. Brené Brown, bestselling author and professor at the University of Houston, talks of courage as "showing one's true heart to others." We can be positive and uplifting in the things we say to people. We can inspire people by spending time to develop their talents. Sometimes being inspiring is as simple as caring about other people more than you care about yourself, maybe listening to them instead of talking. Sometimes being inspiring is being passionate about something. But to be an effective leader at scale, we need to learn how to inspire lots of people simultaneously with a story or picture of the future, a vision.

All effective leaders know that inspiration is valuable as a leadership tool. They realize that some messaging is a pull while other messaging is a push. Pull works better in the long run than push. When you push a little red wagon using the handle, the front end goes in every possible direction, but when you turn the wagon around and pull it, it follows you wherever you go perfectly.

People react similarly: When they are pushed, they become unpredictable. So when you inspire them, you create a pull. Strong, effective leaders recognize this difference and know when to lead from the front and when to lead from the back, as Nelson Mandela expressed it. And they understand that their vision needs to be organized and targeted. Mahatma Gandhi figured out a process for achieving vision through targeted interventions. Winston Churchill developed a formula for communicating and inspiring others with words and speeches. Nelson Mandela wrote about a path for leaders to learn "symbolic" leadership. Martin Luther King Jr., taught that change occurs when the empathetic majority takes up the vision of the minority.

In their own unique circumstances, these leaders needed to "invent" or create an inspiring way that didn't exist to bring their vision closer to reality. For each of these leaders and countless others, there were object lessons and struggles. Each knew that his inner resources would be severely tested in the process. Each grasped he was a symbol of the future to his engaged stakeholders. At some point, every single one of these leaders was not identified by others as a leader. None set out to be leaders. Only in retrospect are they admired, respected, and even mythologized for the ease and simplicity with which they "appeared" to inspire others through their leadership. At the time, things were not so easy or simple for any of them. For all of them, leadership was a messy affair and a learning experience.

Leaders don't often start out as inspirational and uplifting. Being a leader, a purposeful, inspirational leader, is like many skills: It takes time, focus, and dedication.

LEARNING TO BUILD SHARED VISION

James, our Fortune 100 marketing VP, is a numbers-based leader. For him, no messes are allowed. James carefully works through his goals each year by extrapolating the performance of each person and each person's capacity, adding any extra capacity that James thinks he might be able to obtain. When he's done, he cuts everything by 15 percent, ensuring he is able to meet all the goals he has been given. He then hands out everyone's goals and meets with everyone weekly to ensure everybody is on track. He doesn't try to manufacture any inspiration. At this point in his leadership career, he doesn't think about being inspiring or inspiring anyone. It's a numbers game. For James, there are always people, good people, willing to take on these roles just to have a job. At this phase of his development, James is leading from his strength and not necessarily from what will be effective.

Priya, on the other hand, does have a strong sense of what good design and construction look like, and it's a purpose that literally moves with her everywhere she goes. She is constantly watching the construction trades, the popular restaurants, the marquee buildings and stadiums that go up. She and her staff fly all over the world to see what's hot in building designs. Interestingly, it's a vague notion in Priya's mind. Her direct reports constantly talk about design in terms of what Priya would like or would not like. The idea of presenting an idea to her that she would reject is horrifying to each of them. They live and die before each of their showcases to her. Still, over time, each of her direct reports does inevitably build a very strong sense of design, and each ends up building a strong portfolio of successful construction projects.

Priya's process, although occasionally brutal, is frequently successful in building great buildings and great construction leaders. Priya loves to work on inspiring projects. She knows that the work itself can be a source of inspiration, engagement, and innovation. She doesn't believe that she needs to be inspiring, but rather that the work needs to be inspiring. Her Achilles' heel is the uninspiring work that makes up the administrative work in her organization.

In *Jane*'s call center, activity is the master. The brand is well represented, geographies and cultures are well represented, and the phones ring and get answered 24/7. Telemarketers come on and off their shifts, the interviewing center hums with activity, and the football field of a room has a weird sense of quiet. Row after row of cubicles, yet you can barely see anyone. This call center focuses on serving the customers of 24 different business entities. Every team, representing a different entity, wears a different color of sports shirt. Several walls light up with data screens flashing key metrics to the teams so they can see the minute-to-minute results. Multiple times a week, a client-caused crisis arises in multiple teams, and heroic efforts calm the crisis. Jane is rarely out in front of these crises. The patterns of crisis are relatively easy to perceive. However, no overall effort is ever organized to improve the operation. Jane, like James and Priya, is still in learning mode about what does and doesn't work as a leader. She has several years of hard work in front of her. She never intended to run a call center; it was simply a good career move. It wasn't sold to her as an inspiring role either. Her boss told her many times not to take the job because no one else wanted it and there must be something wrong.

James's and Jane's operations are not inspiring places to work. The fundamentals of well-run operations are present, but people come and go. There is no inspiration, no goal bigger than achieving the numbers and getting calls answered on time. In contrast, Priya's operation is built on finding inspiring design and building fascinating buildings, buildings that inspire the people who work on them. Priya fundamentally understands the impact of inspiring work or projects on people, but she personally does not find administrative work inspiring, and she undoes her inspiring leadership with how she treats certain administrative work. It is important to understand that each of these leaders is still a work in progress. At this stage of their careers, they each have focused on what they do well. As they become more effective leaders, they will embrace all the commitments of leadership.

TRANSCENDING WORDS: INSPIRATION AND VISION

In Linkage's research into leadership, the most effective leaders score highest in inspiration. Leaders who put forth broad goals or visions of the future are correspondingly more effective than leaders who don't or who are unclear or ambiguous about their leadership vision.

There are three incontrovertible facts from our research:

- The leader needs to inspire others in order to achieve the goal or vision.

- The leader needs to communicate that goal or vision.

- The more inspiring the language, the more effective the communication.

More so than any other commitment of leadership, the creation of a vision is the least tangible, and maybe for that reason the least understood. However, we all know that leaders own the vision. These visions can be about the significant improvement of the performance of a team, a function, or a company. They can be about a new and more radical product that dramatically improves a customer's life. Maybe the vision can be about how the employees of an organization can better work together to deliver the product, improving their own lives at the same time. Or maybe the vision is to build the organization of the future.

Whatever the vision, can it be stated with clarity and with purpose? Can the vision get past all the noise, all the paradox, and all the legacy that might be getting in the way? It does not matter what we call it: a vision; a big, hairy, audacious goal; a plan; a direction; a future; an intuition or discernment. A vision is a way to picture the future using one's wisdom and imagination. It's a mental image and a point of view about what the future could hold. It's also a bet that leaders are willing to make based on their farsightedness about the conditions of their organization, their industry, and their customers. After all the thinking, the planning, the dreaming, and the hard work of seeing the world as it is and how it could be, the leader must still communicate the vision.

As part of the research, we interviewed a number of leadership experts. There were two strong themes in the data around leadership visions:

- The vision that leaders create must be for something bigger than themselves. The vision must be about making things better for a collective or a community or an organization, not just for the leaders.

- The vision must be ethical and positive. Visions must be optimistic and must be about a common good.

Communicating Your Vision Evocatively

No matter how dry, how mechanical, and how financial a vision may be, it's incumbent on a leader to communicate the goal in a way that inspires people to achieve it.

Visions and goals should not be tyrannical, nor should they be emotionally insipid or extremely difficult to understand and adopt as one's own. A big vision requires the work of many, not just one. It must translate to everyone and be adoptable by everyone. The ownership of the vision by everyone, each in his or her own way, is the foundation for success in leadership. The vision must relate to people on an emotional level to be effective. It needs to be a statement that people passionately embrace as their own.

As a statement, it must be expressive, clear, and compelling while also encouraging and allowing others to feel empowered to stretch for the vision themselves. This one practice, the practice of communicating the vision evocatively, is a function of a person's identity as a leader. Take another look at our automobile mechanic from the Introduction. He was not ready to be a leader, but he communicated the idea of a playground so honestly and so energetically that at least a hundred townsfolk said, "Yeah, I like the idea" and "I can help with that." The simple idea of a playground was something that we all felt was achievable with some work, some planning, and some strong empathy for the children. Clearly, this leader was untrained, inexperienced, and naïve. But we all knew he was leading on behalf of the kids. It was going to be fun!

Providing Goals and Direction

Surprisingly, visions are not specific about what must actually happen. While they point in a compelling direction, they don't tell you what to do to get there. So someone, or everyone, must turn the vision into a set of focused outcomes. Someone needs to come down out of the clouds where the vision resides and put the dream into a set of critical results, key outcomes, or time-based goals. A vision needs a structure; it needs to be embodied into a focused set of actions.

That set of actions is the step that inspires people toward behaviors that create the momentum and energy required to achieve the vision. Oftentimes, when a vision in one person's head gets communicated, it feels as if that vision had been in everyone's head. Consequently, as everyone feels the ownership of the vision, everyone can help to cocreate the goals and outcomes required to achieve it.

Strategic Thinking: A Leadership Skill

Being able to create a vision and then anchor it in goals and direction is a key practice of a leader. Obviously, this is even further anchored in a leader's ability to think critically and creatively or imaginatively. The skill has been described as being able to helicopter from ground-level practical thinking to thinking into the future. It has been described as being able to see the whole and how all the parts relate to that whole. And it has been described as being able to see the disconnect in all the orthodoxy that exists in the way a community of people think about a particular problem or opportunity. Leaders have the capacity to create a framework of decisions that ultimately points in a particular direction. It is a different skill set from what is typically called "problem solving."

In looking at all Linkage's exemplars of purposeful leaders, one thematic skill stood out and underpinned a leader's capability to create a vision: strategic thinking. It even stood out in our statistical analysis of the data: Strategic thinking correlated strongly with creating a vision, and both correlated with leadership effectiveness. This ability to see into the future, or see around corners, is often the cornerstone of the goal and the vision. Strategy is a divergent problem, a problem with no correct solution designed to deal with uncertainty and ambiguity. This makes it a perfect problem for a leader who needs to engage others, use the perspective of others, and garner the engagement of others in the ultimate decision. Dialogue is imperative. Building alignment is critical to success.

Strategic thinking is the ability to assess what is happening with customer needs and wants, competitors' products and services, and the economics of the marketplace—and to develop a solid idea about where you can find an advantage. Strategic thinking is where you find the advantage, not necessarily the idea of the product or the solution primed to innovate. It is a framework for how to look at an opportunity or problem in a way that allows flexibility to solve for that opportunity or problem. After all, leaders are solving for the future in the present—some adaptability is going to be required.

It's safe to say that dynamic strategic thinkers have several practices or habits. They are probably excellent at the simple act of learning multiple perspectives; they listen; they understand the subtle ways that people can be attracted to a product, a service, or an idea; and they are great at testing their ideas with their peers and the public. Strategic thinking also ties into the fundamental skills of any and every leader: judgment and decision making. Suffice it to say, there is no such thing as a problem that is completely technical in nature; people are always involved. People always need to be involved in a solution for it to be implemented. And that is what leadership is really all about—wanting that role of energizing people to a purpose or to goal.

PURPOSE INSIDER

Julia Gillard: One Nation Under a Purposeful Leader

Nowhere do we associate the word "leadership" with a particular arena of life more than we do in the world of politics. Listen to any discussion of government and politics and the word "leadership" will infuse the conversation. Julia Gillard served as Australia's prime minister for three years. She may be best known as a highly skilled negotiator and advocate of a controversial carbon tax, which has increasingly gained more support than opposition. She also pushed to overhaul education funding and provide more benefits and care to people with disabilities. She led her nation as a woman and endured a tremendous amount of criticism due to bias, but she dealt with it all with her sense of purpose. In thinking back, she notes:

> My personal past experience tells me if you go into politics clear about what you're trying to achieve, you get the privilege of forming a government and putting those things into operation. Then you can make a pos-

itive difference and shape the future. I am a believer in the power of government. I'm always keen when I talk to people, particularly young people who are interested in public service and public life, to make sure they have a clear sense of the purpose, the why. Certainly the modern case of politics is so relentless and the media cycle is so fast that if you aren't really clear on what you are trying to achieve, there is every risk you can get pushed off course and do things you hadn't intended to, or not get much done. Clarity of purpose is more important than ever.

Many people have not sat down and developed a clear idea of what they need to do. One thing I did, having been advised by a great friend of mine, was to sit down and write out the purpose of the government I was leading. It was always within easy reach to steady myself and recommit myself to that purpose on difficult days. Lack of clarity about purpose is a big impediment. I think the vast competing demands on people's time and energy distort people from their true purpose. It's not that they're not trying to get things done—it's just that everything else crowds in. Being disciplined about time management and setting aside time to really focus on achieving things that are key to your purpose rather than reacting to things that fill their inbox and fill their diaries is really important. In the world of government, there are many obstacles that push back. Politics is very partisan in this modern age so anyone proposing change can expect to meet opposition and resistance. That opposition and resistance might come from political opponents. It might come from stakeholders. It might come from community groups or sections of the media. You need finely tuned strategies to try to hold as many people with you as you go about the task of change.

"Inspire" speaks to me the most because I come from this life of public advocacy and public policy. You only achieve big things in democracies if you inspire people around a cause. For government, possibly the most challenging is "innovate." The trappings of government, the instrumentalities, the rhythms of governments find it hard to be innovative. One thing putting stresses and strains on democracies now is that they haven't innovated much in a time when so much of the rest of the world has been subject to disruption and innovation, particularly how people get their information today on what is happening in their nation and in their democracy. Government tends to move more slowly and find the innovation challenge harder than many other actors who are more agile.

Governments have pretty low-risk appetites. With the amount of taxpayer scrutiny on every dollar, which is understandable, it is hard for governments to take a risk and try something in which they could fail. The consequences of failure are large indeed in the public realm, whereas agile companies, agile philanthropy can take a risk. It's effective in the risk appetite—if it works, fantastic; if it doesn't, people will

> learn from the failure and go on and do something
> else. That is an accepted reason and approach. That's
> not true with government.

Julia received advice about leadership when she first got into politics, and the advice was probably aimed to help understand the complexity and entrenchment she would experience as she pushed forward. Instead, it served as her foundation, her purpose. She understood who she was and what she was about as a leader. Her deep interests became her platform, and she built a coalition around it. She led from her purpose.

PURPOSE INSIDER

"Psychological Contract to Inspire"

For an organization to achieve anywhere near overall excellence, it takes a number of highly effective leaders at all levels. The College of the Holy Cross in Worcester, Massachusetts, has seen its overall arc of excellence continue to ascend over decades. A big part of this overall arc is Art Korandanis, who after 33 years retired as director of auxiliary services for College of the Holy Cross. He is the first to say that he wants to be remembered for inspiring people. His track record of running college facilities, particularly food service, has been stellar, with his influence of innovative dining programs playing out across many campuses around the country. What was key for keeping his commitment to inspire?

I showed staff the right paths to take. We tried things others didn't. We weren't afraid of failure. I get a thrill from setting the course. Everything I do is about people. I love seeing the best come out of them and putting them in a position that allows them to grow and develop. As a leader, inspiring is figuring out what someone's strengths are and using them in that way. Everyone can be successful. It is a psychological contract that you make with people: Work with me and you will have reasons to stay. Sometimes the most important person in dining is the pot washer; if that person doesn't want to get it done because they're not inspired, you're in trouble. Everyone must feel like part of a team.

Inspiring is sharing your positive thinking and excitement. I put a slow food concept in place in a dining hall. We all sit at the same table for two hours, without cell phones, and talk about new programs while we are eating, drinking, and celebrating. Excitement is the breath of life. Food is exciting.

As my leadership style developed over the years, I've likened it to the way I lead people on hikes in the White Mountains. The hike comes with an overnight stay . . . and a lot of responsibilities. I lead the hikes from behind in a purposeful leadership style: In the beginning, you give everyone a map and define the goal. You communicate transparently that on this hike there will be stream crossings and trail junctions. We'll take breaks. There may be injuries along the way. We discuss the obstacles and decisions that need to be made. I like to do this from behind because I can elect an equally experienced hiker to take us to the point, the destination. I can watch over everyone before each leg of the hike. You build a team as you're following this approach. I make sure everyone is comfortable and give them the option of taking layers off as we build momentum. We need to regroup and talk about what went wrong on a hike—the gear we wish we had brought, the decisions, if everyone held up as they committed to do.

And most importantly, make sure you have wine because you always have to celebrate a job well-done, once you get to the top of the mountain.

Art is very well known in the world of college food service, and so are the people who have worked for him and with him over the years. He has helped many young leaders go from working in his operation to running an operation of their own at another college or university. Art's story not only gives us a great sense of how to lead from behind, but is also a deep view on how, at any given moment, any person could have the most important job in the organization. Art leads by making the goal inspiring and by engaging the talents and the energy of everyone involved. The goal is out front. It is a question of what matters most right then, right there. For Art, leadership is about people, but his ability to inspire people toward a vision or a goal is what stands out for the people around him. He inspires with his vision, his goals, his organization of the path to achieve the goal, and his character as a leader.

PURPOSE INSIDER

Committed to Inspire

There are many paths that leaders can choose to inspire others. There is no recipe. In fact, the idea of there being no recipe might in fact be the recipe. In particular, a no-recipe approach to inspiration probably works best when the leader is working to deepen the appreciation and understanding of a particular set of issues or demands. The vision arises from the dialogue and the inquiry that is part of the process. Kaelyn Phillips of LogMeln compares two leaders who've been inspiring to her:

> They had very different approaches. But they both had a passion. This holds true for those who want to innovate. You are asking a lot. Asking to challenge status quo, get out of your comfort zone. You have to really show that you believe, have a passion. What was different was the way they got me to where they wanted me to go.
>
> In one case I worked with a technology officer, who was the brightest person I have ever met. MBA, Ph.D., brilliant. She would ask for my ideas and then carefully steer me to a more creative approach by asking questions and asking me how I would do it if I were the owner. Then, she unleashed me. I left each conversation feeling like the smartest person in the world. I would get back to my desk. And I would get

an email that she had pre-written. She knew how to inspire me and get me out of my comfort zone.

The other set the expectation that we would not do the status quo. He would ask, "Is this different? Is this unique?" He would get there the same way as the CTO. He was more accepting. She was more directive.

Both of them are, by nature, creative. They do not think about status quo. They come to the table wanting to do something different. They push and make it clear that they are not thinking of the ordinary and are looking for you to step up. For her, she just sees things in a different way. I would imagine she is very visual. In her mind, anything can be accomplished. What she sees she can make happen, because it is what she asked for. For him, it was more about adapting to understand what is needed. He has worked in a lot of roles in many orgs. Thus, he understands there are lots of paths to get there. When you have had six different roles in six years, you are going to have a different mindset than someone who has been in the same position for six years. By adapting, he adapted his mindset.

What's interesting about Kaelyn's different examples of inspiration is they both involved investigating and setting a future picture, building understanding and clarity, gaining her buy-in, setting some aspirational expectations, and guiding Kaelyn along the way with some very practical rituals.

FROM PURPOSE TO MASTERY

Becoming a leader is a journey over time. It is a journey in how to make change real. Leaders create or help create a vision. They build an organization around the vision (and themselves) to energize and structure the path to that vision. They create the necessary climate and focus so that key areas of the organization can innovate in critical ways to achieve that vision. And they organize people, processes, technology, and money to ensure that the goal has the best possible chance of being achieved. Good visions clearly separate what the future will look like compared with the current state. Visions create a tension with the current state that must be resolved. When we are guided by vision, we get up every day asking ourselves what needs to happen to make that vision a reality. Visions may describe the future, but they are successful when they change what is happening now. Visionary organizations are not stable; they are constantly changing and striving to be more like their own vision of the future. They understand that they are moving toward something better for themselves, their customers, and their stakeholders.

As we shall see in the next chapters, leaders' visions come from their life experiences, their sense of ethics and fairness, their sense of right and wrong, their discernment of a problem or an issue that no one else can see, or even their simple belief in the future being better than today. Visions come from the leaders' experiences of "what is" and evolve into "what could be." From there, they are refined and honed and tuned. My mentor Donella Meadows used to say, "Great goals change everything."

VISION PROBE

- What inspires you to get out of bed every day and go to work?

- When you do get out of bed every day, whom do you inspire?

- Are you, as a leader, a role model? Caring? A developer of your people? Courageous? A good listener? Passionate about something? A person who spreads positivity?

- What would you like to see different as a result of your leadership? Set a time frame—for example, three years. What will be different in the team, function, or company where you lead in three years because you were leading it? What do you have energy around? Confidence around? Optimism around?

- What would it look like to have the people in your organization say that they are inspired by the vision?

- What would an inspiring message look like, sound like, and feel like to someone listening to your vision?

- What vision could you create that would have the room to allow others the freedom to cocreate that dream?

- What vision would allow others to feel success and recognition as well?

- How could your vision be wrong? Where might others be able to help cocreate a better vision?

- What would bring strategic, competitive advantage to your organization?

- How could you develop the habit or ritual of repeating the vision over and over again so that you feel the energy, the positivity, and the authenticity of the vision? How could you feel confident that the vision is the best thing for everyone?

- If you could script the critical moves to achieve the vision, what would those moves be? How could these moves become goals?

4

THE BIG WHY: HOW TO CONNECT YOU AND YOUR CONTEXT

For me, becoming isn't about arriving somewhere or achieving a certain aim. I see it instead as forward motion, a means of evolving, a way to reach continuously toward a better self. The journey doesn't end. I became a mother, but I still have a lot to learn from and give to my children. I became a wife, but I continue to adapt to and be humbled by what it means to truly love and make a life with another person. I have become, by certain measures, a person of power, and yet there are moments still when I feel insecure or unheard. It's all a process, steps along a path. Becoming requires equal parts patience and rigor. Becoming is never giving up on the idea that there's more growing to be done.

—*Michelle Obama, First Lady of the United States (2009–2017)*

BORN THIS WAY?

A leader's most important ability is their capacity to take people to a different place, to a world of new opportunities. Leaders are the stewards of a vision and the long-term perspective. Interestingly, as long as I've been in the field of leadership, no one has ever said to me that it is his or her true calling to organize people around a vision. What drives people to believe so much in something that they build, or enlist, a collection of talented people to shape that vision into a real possibility? What choices need to be made? What support is required? What experiences are important?

James, Priya, and Jane are becoming leaders. They each have the confidence and support of their executive leadership. They each are in a different place in their leadership. James and Jane are still trying to find themselves and their leadership. Priya has found her purpose, but she has trouble finding an organization where she is truly aligned.

When I first met *James*, he was the perfect representation of this story of leadership becoming. He had graduated from a great college in the middle of his class. He largely worked his way through college as a work-study student. First he worked in the cafeteria, then he worked in the library. By his senior year he was the lead student on the late-night and weekend shifts at the library. People would often look at him in bewilderment when he said it (and he said it often), "You wouldn't believe what happens in a college library late at night!" James learned to deal with a spectrum of human events, both positive and negative. He even wrote a series of short fictional stories for the college literary magazine playing out some of the scenarios. He majored in marketing and was hired out of university by an online retailer. Unfortunately, he had to deal with the death of his father shortly before his graduation. His father was an accountant who had partnered with several college friends to form an accounting firm in a medium-sized Eastern city dominated by financial institutions. His dad had done well and led an extremely traditional life. His death came as a shock to everyone.

After struggling with early challenges, James was given a project to manage by his boss's boss, and James hit a home run, despite some occasional interference from his direct boss. This led to several other larger and more significant projects. James developed a number of key competencies from these projects: He mastered the project update, the project kick off, budget management, resource allocation, and the software development project as well as managing the scores of types of information available from various marketing systems. When James's mentor left the online organization, he quickly hired James to join him at the new company that offered a substantial jump in responsibility.

James quickly gained a reputation for being focused, outcome-driven, and ambitious. What surprised him was his growing competence in working with numbers. He had never shown any talent for math or calculus in school. He had always been teased and chided by his father that he wasn't going to take over his spot in the accounting firm. Out of nowhere, James developed a facility to look at large, complicated spreadsheets and find errors and problems almost without looking at the spreadsheet. He would both shock and intimidate his direct reports with his expertise around the numbers. His depth of understanding was firmly rooted in the math and the economics of marketing. Along with his growing expertise came an unsympathetic and judgmental fault-finding with others. He also developed an impatience with everyone around him. But he got things done.

As his reputation grew, he was finally lured away from his mentor to a Fortune 500 organization as one of three marketing leaders reporting to the chief marketing officer. With more than 100 direct reports, James had lots of responsibility, but he had no emotional connection to the company or the industry. From the outside, all that could be seen was ambition—something his new boss greatly admired. James became someone people wanted to attach themselves to. They could see a rising star, and they wanted to be a part of his organization. He began to develop a core group of followers with deep expertise in specific areas of marketing. Together they started to create a culture of performance excellence. Although there were clearly some core issues and dilemmas of concern to everyone with how this was happening, James's boss was clearly reveling in the results that were being achieved. James and his crew had developed a capability to foresee issues months in advance of others and take advantage of the opportunities in those issues. Their marketing initiatives had the hallmark of being prescient. As James entered his late thirties, he was making a great salary, was clearly earmarked for great things, and was a workaholic.

Priya had taken a different path to becoming. She knew early she wanted to be a structural engineer and won a scholarship to a highly prestigious East Coast engineering school. The daughter of an engineer, she was a fast study in the classroom and a tireless networker. Schoolwork didn't exactly come easy to her, but she was extremely diligent and thorough in her preparation and study. Priya didn't nail her tests; she overwhelmed them with preparation. She often took professors to task for asking bad questions on tests or grading answers lazily. She would argue, defend, and prove a professor wrong when she felt a professor had graded a test incorrectly or a question was ambiguous enough to be answered several different ways. She took every opportunity available to meet industry notables, hear them speak at lectures, and talk to them at cocktail parties, even if it meant she was a server at the party. She knew all her classmates and cultivated strong relationships with her professors. She graduated near the top of her class.

After graduation she moved quickly into a prized internship with a leading engineering company. The company hired her, and she quickly rose into a responsible and visible position. Priya was constantly finding new ways to make things happen and was extremely successful in her choices. When her construction firm was bought out by another firm, she decided to leave and pursue a master's degree, attending a prestigious engineering program on the West Coast. She returned to business and landed the role of project leader with a major family-owned construction firm. In this role, she saw how she could impact results by having a strong group of equally talented engineers working for her, and she developed an eye for talent. She loved to work with younger talent like herself. Priya had a strong ability to communicate what kinds of designs and processes were going to work with customers. She had a strong predictive sense of what was going to happen and where there were risks and opportunities on a project, and she could communicate it in metaphors and analogies. She knew everyone in the industry and was constantly and consciously, in a disciplined manner, cultivating everybody's intuition as well. She took risks, and they paid off. She even managed to personally succeed when one or two of her projects suffered from contentious and unsuccessful design problems. The clients she worked for continued to support her and demanded she lead their projects. This did not go over as well inside her own firm. She was the only woman at her level, and her peers often made life difficult for her. When clients stuck by her and showed tremendous loyalty to her, things got worse for her internally. It didn't help that many of the younger, more talented engineers also wanted to work for her over some of her peers.

After a few years, Priya decided to pursue an MBA and attended probably the most prestigious MBA program in the country. She surprised everyone when she returned to her old firm. Suddenly, what she said carried a lot of influence organizationally. Essentially, she influenced a major reorganization of the firm into specialty segments focused on distinct types of construction. Everyone in the firm went from building everything to specializing in different construction scenarios. However, Priya was not on the executive team and not a family member. She was tossed into the organizational fray just like everyone else despite having played a major role in conceptualizing the new strategy and organization design. When everything was settled, she ended up working for a family member in the largest division of the company. She was the de facto leader of the division, and she resented having to report to the family member.

Priya had always shown a love for the technical side of the business: the design process, the engineering process, the construction process, and the client relationship process. But she never really got used to the organizational processes—what she called the bureaucracy. She always felt that organizational processes were about negative goals or defensive goals, and they created a disproportionate amount of unnecessary work as well. Priya knew pretty much everyone in construction for a good 150-mile radius, so when she needed to hire someone, she knew exactly the people she was looking for and knew exactly how to get to them. She saw no use for résumés, interviews, reference calls, and all the work that a hiring manager had to go through to make a good hire. For Priya, the best people often didn't even apply. She saw most organizational and financial processes similarly. She had no patience for them, and she would overwhelm the process owners with her critiques of their process, just as she had overwhelmed her professors in college. She was unrelenting and harsh at times. Still, the executives saw her as the rising star in the organization. Clients loved her, architects loved her, contractors preferred to build for her over others in the firm, and key talent in the organization wanted to work for her. The members of the executive team felt that they could easily smooth off her rough edges.

Jane took yet another way in her journey to leadership. Jane graduated from a state university with distinction in a liberal arts major but struggled to find a job after college. During her college years she had worked as a tutor in the student association, eventually ending up running the entire operation of more than 100 tutors. She excelled at matching tutors with students, finding the right pairing to make it work. She managed the recruiting process for tutors, she managed the budget, and she developed a system to measure quality.

Jane's career struggle after college continued for more than six months, but she eventually found work as a teller at a large bank. She was out of her realm, and she overcompensated by becoming the best teller at her branch. She didn't really make friends. Ultimately, she did get noticed and promoted to a regional office overseeing teller operations. As an individual contributor, she often audited branches and teller operations. She learned the business. She built a reputation around knowing every process and every procedure. When a supervisory position opened up in the bank's call center, she applied and won the job. In her new position, she relied heavily on her expertise and grew into a warm, humble, yet firm manager. As Jane grew, her growth was always biased toward the operations side of the business, not toward the organizational side of things. She never really learned how to hire, fire, develop, engage, and mentor others.

Since she operated as an individual contributor for most of her career, she was good at keeping to herself, but she was an expert trainer. Jane found herself getting multiple promotions, and when the call center leader left due to an illness, Jane was promoted to lead the entire call center, more than 100 phone reps, 8 supervisors and managers, and 4 directors reporting to her. She inherited an organization that struggled to make things work: constantly under-staffed and undertrained, barely meeting standards, dealing with a growing number of customer issues, and relying too often on hero-ics to get by. It was a not a good organization and was plagued by multiple legal issues as well. Interestingly, she also took over just as the bank went on an acquisition spree. Integrating new banks into her call center became routine, and her operation exploded in size in her first year.

James, Priya, and Jane are in their positions of leadership because of what they know and because of who they are as people. They are secure in their domain expertise. They are still caught up in the what of their expertise. They are still trying to find their pur-pose as a leader.

———

Are leaders made or born? How do leaders become leaders? How does someone become inspiring, engaging, innovative, and pur-poseful? While all leaders are born, have parents and grandpar-ents, and thus certain attributes; its our experiences and values that really shape us. Fortunately, these attributes, values, and behaviors are what get us noticed in our organizations and our communi-ties. When we reflect a certain set of values and principles, the cur-rent leaders of the organization notice us. They pick us out and give us opportunities to be a team leader or a project leader. We get a chance to show what we can do, and in the process we gain valu-able experience. Now, let's be honest; a bias exists in the way this relationship probably developed. It's likely that the leaders chose a young person like a Jane or a James that looked like them, valued the same things that they did, and had many of the same basic personality characteristics. But again, opportunity knocks and experience, valuable leadership experience, is gained.

FROM INDIVIDUAL CONTRIBUTOR TO LEADER

In reviewing our leadership exemplars, we saw several major patterns in how leaders grow and develop over time. What was distinctive about the patterns is that, while each individual leader exhibited a different individual paths, we saw many of the same basic patterns. As James, Priya, and Jane all exemplify, we saw eight major clusters of developmental experiences.

1. **EARLY LEADERSHIP EXPERIENCE.** A significant percentage of the leaders we looked at in our exemplars had significant leadership experiences early in their careers. Often these experiences involved a mentor, a sponsor, and unusual amounts of responsibility for their age and level of experience.

2. **COMPETENCY ACQUISITION.** Although we couldn't find a pattern, developing leaders acquired and built distinct complexes of competence. They didn't build skills in isolation of each other; they built networks of competence that were more holistic in nature.

3. **THE ART OF GOAL SETTING.** Leadership is more than just making sure that things work well or that the team is executing. It's more than just preserving the core. As Jim Collins stated so well, "Leadership is about stimulating

progress." They are strategists, change agents, and consultants when they are able to work with a group of people and find the right goal for the organization to pursue. They learn to set goals for a team of five, for a function of fifty, or for extremely large organizations of people across all sorts of cultures and boundaries.

4. **LEADERS LEARNING TO EXECUTE AGAINST THE GOALS.** It's one thing to develop goals, and a great many leaders are able to articulate great goals. It's quite another to develop the capability to organize people, processes, and systems, together with standards of quality, and create momentum toward the goals. It's also quite a feat to do this with five people, fifty people, five hundred people, and even five thousand or more people. What's more, in our use cases, we saw execution differ by company and by industry. Structuring people into organized groups that communicate with others, build feedback loops with each other, develop processes with multiple handoffs between teams and functions, and shape the culture that surrounds all this—that's learning to execute.

5. **LEADERS BECOMING PURPOSEFUL.** Becoming is best expressed for me in Joseph Campbell's book *The Hero's Journey*. Real heroes go on a journey, and the real journey isn't the physical challenge. The true journey is the internal challenge, the intuitiveness, and the boredom that results from doing something every day for 10 years to make something work. The real journey is what goes on inside a person. As Joseph Jaworski, author of *Synchronicity* and founder of the American Leadership Forum, says,

"Leadership is an offer of a relationship around a future; it is a call to action."

6. **GOALS BECOMING VISIONS.** Eventually, leaders build a larger and more futuristic view of the world that they live in as leaders. When we talk about discernment and vision, it's the ability to know what your customers need down the road and to know what gaps exist in your industry in such a way that you could put forward a goal or idea that fills the gap before your competitors do. A visionary is someone who pushes forward a product or set of ideas long before customers know they need it. Leaders know the industry is not developing these things.

7. **LEADERS LEARNING TO LEAD TEAMS.** It was clear in the developmental path of every one of our leaders that leading a team was a big part of the learning to lead. Finding the right diverse mix of individuals and building them into a collective that "thought together" was more challenging to learn how to do than anyone would have predicted. It is difficult to get past each person's individual agenda, keep people's ambitions in check, support the quieter team members, and help the team to build on each other's thinking. The dynamics of teams are extremely challenging to learn.

8. **LEADERS LEARNING TO BUILD AND SUPPORT LEADERS.** What became clear in our research is that all leaders reach a point in their business or organizational life when what they want to accomplish requires the engagement not of team members, but of other leaders. At some point, every leader has to learn to let others take up the responsibility,

the communication, the organization, and the execution of major pieces of the goal. Of course, the best way to accomplish this is to build leaders who are as deeply committed to the goal as you are yourself. You can't hire leaders who are only good at leading and merely compliant when it comes to the vision, instead of fully embracing it.

Although our leadership exemplars showed us these eight patterns, they showed us no discernible pattern of how individuals acquired these eight major experiences. In fact, some effective leaders were missing one or two of these. What really threw us for a loop was that some leaders became effective in leading without any of these experiences. There are many myths about leaders and leadership. It's such a complex behavior, this capability to inspire people to achieve a vision or goal. But this complexity leads to misconceptions and misunderstanding. Ultimately, however, the leaders without any of these experiences had a strong sense of purpose that had developed over years or even decades. We couldn't find the experience, but we did find the sense of purpose.

PURPOSE INSIDER

Carla Harris: Always Arriving

Carla Harris is a vice chairman, managing director, and senior client advisor at Morgan Stanley. She is responsible for increasing client connectivity and penetration to enhance revenue generation across the firm. Previously, she headed the Emerging Manager Platform, the equity capital markets effort for the consumer and retail industries, and was responsible for equity private placements. In her 30-year career, Harris has had extensive industry experiences in the technology, media, retail, telecommunications, transportation, industrial, and healthcare sectors. In August 2013, Harris was appointed by President Barack Obama to chair the National Women's Business Council. As an accomplished author, singer, and speaker, Harris has a lot to say about purposeful leadership:

> "Become" is that you never have arrived. While you may get to a space where you are qualified to lead, if you are smart, you will always learn. By definition, you are becoming something else. You are becoming a seasoned leader. You are becoming a better leader. You are becoming a mature leader. After I thought about the principles more, "become" made a lot of sense to me. Essentially, you are agreeing that you are always going to evolve. Every time I hear a great leader speak, I hear them say that they are naturally curious. They are somebody who is always seeking out something.
>
> Obviously, "inspire" and "achieve" are things you have to do, especially when you first acquire a leadership role. Usually, you acquire a leadership role because you put some points on the board. In a producer culture, that is tricky because some leaders have been awarded roles because they are great producers. That does not mean that person is going to end up being a great leader or a great manager. They have just been a great producer. In a producer culture, you reward people with seats of leadership, position,

power, influence as a result of their accomplishments. However, this is not the way we're going to be able to do things in the future. If you think about what Millennials and Z'ers require, they want to be led, managed, inspired, motivated.

The younger generation has expressed they want purpose and meaning in life early on, which is something you didn't hear Boomers say. You saw them [Boomers] struggle with this when they were about to retire after doing something for twenty-five or thirty years. "What does all this mean? I have acquired stuff—experience, titles, material things—but what imprint have I made on the world?" It used to be that charitable organizations didn't want you to be engaged until you had arrived at a certain level of competency or earnings. Now you find a nonprofit organization actively soliciting young talent, young energy. Purpose is something important around the world. It is a thing that anchors your "why." Why are you doing what you are doing? Why are you working as hard as you are working? Why are you investing money? Time mentoring this person? People have realized that without a purpose, it is hard to stay connected to that driver, especially in tough economic times or when things get personally challenging.

Understand *why* you are doing what you're doing. No matter what, it will anchor you and allow you to be focused and persevere. Even when you're thinking about the broader picture, think about what you're

passionate about so you can have some of it intention-
ally in your world. Purpose continues to evolve for me.
Early on, my passion, my purpose, was to be a great
banker. Why? No. 1, I wanted to do well at whatever
I had chosen to do. No. 2, I knew there weren't a lot
of people that look like me that were out there doing
it. No. 3, I knew I had the power to open the door for
other people. No. 4, I had to support the people who
were already there trying to get it done and pass along
my learning of how to be successful. Now, 31 years
later, I say to myself, "I may have been a great banker,
but boy, am I a really great speaker." Now I also say to
myself, "Wait! I thought it was this thing, but maybe
it's this other thing!" That is the thing about evolving. If you had told me 30 years ago, "Carla, your voice
is going to be important in the world," I would have
thought you meant my singing voice. I had no idea it
would be my speaking voice. It wasn't until recently
that I've had this epiphany around: Wait a minute . . .
hold on, Carla, there is something special over here.
You should pay attention. Your purpose and your
"aha" moment can evolve as you grow and evolve.

Carla is explicit about the reasons many become leaders, and it
isn't because they have leadership potential. She is also explicit that
leadership is about finding your purpose, finding your voice, and
most especially finding your uniqueness, which will evolve as you
gain clarity about your passion.

PURPOSE INSIDER

Richard Leider, founder of Inventure— The Purpose Company

Richard Leider, consistently ranked a top executive life coach by Forbes and Conference Board for more than four decades, breathes purpose in and out of his every step in life, and of course, not without helping tens of thousands of others unlock and serve their own purpose in the process. He does not see successful leadership without the installation of purpose at every decision and strategy:

Why do we have leaders? What do they actually provide that is useful? Consider great leaders you have known, either personally or in your study of leadership. When you think about these leaders at a high level, what do they provide to their followers and organizations?

The value of leaders is to engage and to boost the well-being of people at work, in the broadest sense. The best leaders I have known account for the broader influence they have on their followers and the networks that surround them. Employees can only fully engage if the leader has a heart, which goes beyond income. Leaders bring who they are to what they do and tend to care about those around them. Some leaders will ignore employee well-being, as if it is beyond their job, but they do so at their peril. To be competitive, you have to care.

The ultimate challenge is self leadership. Self leadership is the primary source of power, not position, intellect, or technical knowledge. Intelligence and technical skills matter, but self is what really matters. I challenge you to go there, and self leadership is hard to measure. It's leadership presence. It's not "dressing for success," but performing with mastery—that is presence, and it entails seven areas:

- **A CENTERED PRESENCE.** Staying grounded in what we care about, but also with the person. People have a yearning for connection.

- **CAPACITY TO GENERATE, RECEIVE, AND FIX TRUST WHEN IT IS BROKEN.** Admit mistakes, even as a leader.

- **EMPATHY AND RESPECT.** This is where purpose comes in. There is a sense of dignity and respect for the humanity in others.

- **BEING ABLE TO LISTEN.** Those who listen have the real power. This is the one core capacity.

- **KNOWLEDGE OF WHAT IT IS TO BE AUTHENTIC.** This is another area where purpose comes in: to lead from your own sense of values. This is what is needed to be trusted by others. Leaders must walk the talk and come from their core.

- **ABILITY TO COORDINATE EFFECTIVELY WITH OTHERS.** Maybe this is "teaming"? Are we on the same page with others? Is the team on the same page?

- **A DESIRE TO BE A LIFELONG LEARNER.** Things have become more complicated. Be a student of leadership and listen. Leaders are only as good as their practices. I used to work with Stephen Covey, author of *The Seven Habits of Highly Effective People.* He said leadership is "common sense," and we are teaching "common practice."

According to Leider, to Covey's way of thinking, we are codifying leadership practice by helping people to be ethically alert, thoughtful, and reflective; being able to understand and appreciate the nuances in leadership choices; and being humble.

Richard Leider frequently cites his mentor, Viktor Frankl, as the inspiration for some of his talks and life's work. We also respect and reference Frankl as we dive into the collective story of purposeful leadership.

Though an inmate himself at a concentration camp during the Holocaust, Frankl at first worked as a physician until he was assigned to provide therapy to new inmates to help them overcome the shock and horror of internment. Many were dealing with how to cope and just get through the ordeal.

I can't imagine how difficult it would be to be a therapist in a concentration camp. What hope could you offer patients? What arguments could you make to improve their outlook on life? Those inmates were experiencing extreme cruelty and unbelievable hardship. Life was random, cheap, and practically meaningless. Imagine yourself in such a position. Your oppressors are monsters. The world outside the camp seems largely indifferent to your fate. Your fellow inmates can't always be trusted; some will do anything to survive. Even your faith in God is brutally tested. What divinity would allow such horror to happen?

Viktor Frankl was one of those who did not lose all hope or heart, even though he lost so much else, including his own wife and parents. Immediately after rescue, he began to write about and assess what he had seen— not the cruelty, violence, and horror of the camps, but the reactions to it all, the way people coped, and the stages they went through in adapting to their circumstances.

His arresting book, *Man's Search for Meaning*, is a portrait of the human condition. In his book, Frankl writes that everyone went through similar phases of despondency in the camps and, perhaps more interestingly, when returning to the world. These emotions were characterized by shock or numbness, bitterness, anger, and a sense of having no control or agency over one's own life. He determined that there was a key difference between people who succumbed and people who survived. The survivors had a strong, perhaps innate, sense of meaning and purpose. They found meaning even in life's seemingly insignificant moments: a kind word, the taste of food, a pleasant dream, a view of the sky. They found purpose—the need to get more food, the need to live another day, the need to tell the world what was happening, the need to save a loved one— even when it may have been delusional to be optimistic. In other words, the people who were oriented toward a positive and meaningful future were able to summon the resources, strength, spirit, generosity, creativity, and will to survive.

Few of us have experienced anything close to the horror of a concentration camp, and of course, the business world is nothing like the Holocaust. Yet at an emotional level, we can all relate to the trials Frankl describes. In surviving tragedy, whether large or small, the mind, spirit, and body adapt to shock and grief in remarkably similar ways. The loss can be a loved one, a home, a precious belonging, a treasured circumstance, a key role, or even an intangible dream. We are in strong agreement with Frankl's conclusions about the vital importance of meaning and purpose in the lives we lead—no matter what circumstance we find ourselves in. When we have meaning and purpose, we are clearer about what we want and who we are, and we are less likely to settle for what we don't want. If we do settle, we have a better understanding of why.

Ordinary life, while less marked by tragedy, can also be difficult to navigate successfully.

Expectations, limitations, and hardships are easy to give in to, especially when we lack a sense of meaning and purpose. The "whatever" way of life may be less real than a prison guard who beats us; yet like any nightmare, it's a monster of our own making. In the end, all of us will face hardships and have to cope with formidable challenges and sometimes fall victim to fate.

Giving in or giving up on something dear to us is a sure road to despondency—while not settling is a determination followed by a plan. It can create road maps to new beginnings.

We should never forget that it is our dreams that keep us focused on a higher purpose and that from purpose we find meaning. The route to a fulfilling life is to figure out how to keep our dreams in order. The best way to do this is with a plan. If we are not careful, we will be asked to settle—perhaps for less than what we want. Each of us must determine what we won't settle for and create a road map to be sure we get the best opportunity.

The antidote for staving off settling for less than what is important is passion. When we are fired up with resolve, we now believe we trigger gene expressions that wire together many genes to create meaning. The way to stay in control of our lives is to be crystal clear about purpose, so that meaning drives accelerated gene activity. While the neuroscience and biology of leadership is still a big question mark, we know that our passions can generate physical and neurological responses in our body and that there is a feedback cycle back to our passions.

What is in the leader that makes him or her exude a sense of purpose and integrity? Leider adds:

> It is the softest of the soft. It makes everyone feel like they are contributing to something that matters, the thread of purpose from the top to the bottom. You make a difference. For too many employees, the return on emotional equity is near zero. At its essence: to reach beyond ourselves to do something that matters, to do something more at work. It helps people feel like they know how they fit. The bottom line is that to succeed, the great leader provides people a way to bring

their humanity to work. I would call them authentic, which breeds trust and charisma. It generates emotional connection. A big part of the purposeful leader is their ability to be reflective in that they assess mistakes and successes.

The essence of Richard Leider's lifetime of work is a critical part of purposeful leadership. So much of what he has learned and talks about is the depth of emotion, understanding, and reflection that it takes to be a highly effective purposeful leader.

COMMITTED TO INSPIRE

Tham Chien Ping is head of the APAC region for Boehringer Ingelheim, one of the largest pharmaceutical companies in the world. In describing leaders, he notes:

One other thing that might be missing is not so much the leader output but learning agility: How to get leaders to continuously learn and grow themselves. Some leaders think they're already there and they know enough. If they think that way, they're finished. How do you get a leader who has been in the job for twenty years to learn from a person who just joined the organization? It's human nature for a person to fall back on what they are comfortable with and what has helped them be successful.

Credibility resonates with me because at the end of the day it's about whether people believe you. It's only when you are credible and consistent in what you do, and you can show an example of how you've done it, that you're able to build a personal brand. So credibility is all about consistency of action and the personal brand that comes with it. You can only lead/ inspire others with credibility.

Tham Chien Ping illustrates and emphasizes that leadership is a responsibility for others and that trust and credibility deepen that responsibility.

Christian Chao of United Overseas Bank emphasizes certain behaviors leaders exhibit: being proactive and taking initiative:

We now live in a time where all employees are expected to behave this way. So what I'm sharing are the unique behaviors and challenges that leaders need to address.

One simple definition is that leaders are there to encourage people to go places they wouldn't go alone. If people are happy to go somewhere, you don't need a leader. But where there's fear or lack of confidence or lack of ability, leaders play an important role. So, what roles can they play?

- **LEADERS PROVIDE A SENSE OF CONFIDENCE IN PEOPLE.** If we unpack confidence here, it can be achieved by the leader providing clarity. As a follower, I know my leader has clarity on where we need to go as an organization. So I have confidence that he'll take us there. And clarity comes from being able to communicate well, having a vision, all those different ingredients to providing clarity.

- **LEADERS MUST EXHIBIT COURAGE.** That comes about when the leader is willing to take risks and take steps that employees may not take themselves. Leaders confront difficult issues, and seeing leaders do that gives the team the courage to then take those steps, even at some personal cost. The leader is usually the one who has to take the biggest risk.

- **LEADERS INSPIRE AND CREATE A SENSE OF MEANING FOR THE WORK THAT PEOPLE DO.** You're not going to take a risk unless it is something that has real value. A good leader is one who is able to expand that value and meaning to the team. For example, if the team thinks this is great for us as a team to reach these KPIs, then leaders will need to go beyond themselves or the organization or the community. So the leader is always stretching to a bigger vision.

These are the three broad, unique responsibilities/ expectations. The leader's personality and the context in which he operates will determine the how of leadership.

What do we stand for? What defines us? Leaders are there to create outcomes that are good for the organization. To do that, you need to be responsible for everyone. A corollary to responsibility is being authentic with your feelings, being vulnerable and open. That can be a struggle.

As leaders, what impact can we make? I'm also looking for leverage to create a big outcome. Leaders should focus on outcomes. What makes the leader is the outcome, not looking internally or navel gazing. A leader is a leader because there's a difference to be made.

Leaders need to have a solid ethical anchor and have character and courage to make critical decisions. If they make poor decisions, that can damage organizations and communities. So, as leadership development experts, as we try to mass-produce leaders, we need to demonstrate that ethical backbone ourselves.

Even though we have said it before, it's important to remember that at its heart, leadership is about means and outcomes. Finding the right way to implement a strategy with people to achieve something purposeful takes being reflective, exploring choices, and making sure that you know what you are trying to achieve. Leadership is a struggle.

GROWTH PROBE

- What do you believe that you do well as a leader?

- Ask 10 people to give you a few one-word adjectives that describe you as a leader.

- What is your sense of identity as a leader? Without using any outside opinions, write 10 adjectives that describe you as a leader.

- What are your most pressing leadership challenges? How do these relate to the challenges that the organization is experiencing?

- Describe the leader you hope never to become.

- Describe why you lead.

PART THREE

ENGAGE

5

ABOUT OTHERS: ENGAGE AND GATHER THE TEAM

Good leaders make people feel that they're at the very heart of things, not at the periphery. Everyone feels that he or she makes a difference to the success of the organization. When that happens people feel centered and that gives their work meaning.

—*Warren G. Bennis, scholar, organizational consultant, and author*

COMMITMENT: ENGAGE

Identify and offer opportunities to engage, contribute, and thrive at work.

Climate change is a controversial issue: many do not believe the climate is changing, and others do not believe any change in the climate is caused by humans. You can find a spectrum of people on both issues. And while the world is adjusting its behavior to create more sustainability, it may not be enough or be fast enough to make a difference in what may be happening.

As the world grapples with this issue, a teenager from Sweden, Greta Thunberg, has become a symbol of environmental activism. By starting a school strike for the climate and inspiring and engaging hundreds of thousands of schoolchildren around the world, she has changed the conversation about the future of our planet. Her single day of protest has turned into a million-plus schoolchildren joining to protest the current politics of sustainability. She has engaged schoolchildren, environmentalists, politicians, businesses, and international institutions in her cause, turning them into both witting and unwitting allies by inspiring a different conversation and actions. She is a symbol and a lightning rod for accelerated action on climate change and a new type of politics.

Greta engages with a purpose. She has studied as much about climate change as most adults knowledgeable about the subject. She speaks with clarity and force about the crisis and solutions. She role models a sustainable life. She has borrowed the tactics and strategies of successful civil disobedience and innovated on them. She is extraordinarily candid. She has faced criticism, resistance, and pressure—even from her own parents. All the while her movement has engaged people in 71 countries and over 700 different cities. She has no organization and no subordinates; what she has are followers: people who want the same goal as she does and feel empowered to take action. Her critics attack her and belittle her, she is unfazed. She leads with focus and purpose.

Why do people follow a leader? Why do people follow you as a leader? What do they see in you that creates engagement in them? How do you go from an individual who spots an opportunity, turns it into a goal, and uses that goal to inspire others to engage as fully in attaining the goal as you do? How do you turn one (yourself) into many? What do people see in you? What do you see in them? Do you have a purpose that inspires and communicates to others?

LEADER IN NAME ONLY

Let's momentarily look at this from the other side. There's a disparaging phrase that is sometimes used in organizations to describe a leader as an "empty suit." The phrase is meant to define a leader who lacks substance or ability. Even worse, it depicts a leader who overestimates his or her ability and importance while in reality having no impact on the situation or others. Although the remark is largely aimed at incompetence, the essence of the remark is really aimed at the lack of character or purpose of the leader.

The empty suit leader is the leader in name or title only. There are no followers. There is no relationship between the leader and followers; the feedback loop that should exist is absent. The multiplying, amplifying effect of the feedback loop is nonexistent. There's no beat or pulse to the feedback loop. The cycle of leader and follower each upping each other's game does not exist.

Engagement is often described as the way people bring themselves to the mission, vision, and values of an organization. It is the employee's commitment and connection to the organization. Consequently, plenty of research supports the conclusion higher levels of engagement promote or support customer loyalty, organi-

zational outcomes, and business value. The importance of engagement has risen to the point where we also develop best practices to
drive employee engagement. There are multiple types of engagement best practices:

- Loyalty

- Productivity

- Emotional connection with the company

- Motivation to succeed

- The willingness to speak positively about the organization

- The strength of one's desire to stay at the organization

- The voluntary, discretionary effort an employee exhibits

Organizations spend millions of dollars surveying, assessing,
and measuring their employee engagement. Without spending too
much time on the research, there is plenty of evidence we as leaders
are not doing a great job engaging our followers. Several credible,
well-known surveys put global workforce engagement at less than
20 percent. That means that one in five people that work around
you or with you is truly connected to what he or she does every day.
It means that four out of five people you work with are less than
productive, may speak poorly of the company outside of work, and
won't give you anything extra.

MASTERING ENGAGEMENT

James has never been called an empty suit, but most of his direct
reports are not in a position to have a difficult conversation with

him, or challenge him, or really help his leadership efforts. James is a focused individual who directs all his direct reports' time and energy, which is a funny way to say that he micromanages. He has a strong reputation as a marketing professional, and people come to work for him expecting to learn the ins and outs of marketing. They learn, and they move on. James takes advantage of this classroom by being choosy about his direct reports. He hires the best and demands they produce. Where James succeeds in engaging others is with his peers and his superiors. They all view his expertise and command of his marketing domain as magical. They love his intensity and his focus. They count on him.

Priya is also not an empty suit. She inspires many to go into the construction industry, and she has strong loyalty from many of the individuals who work for her. As a female in a mostly male industry, she is an attractor for her firm. In addition, her company uses her to recruit other female talent. She is demanding, and the people who don't measure up to her standards quickly disengage and eventually find their way out of her organization.

Jane drives her team crazy with her blind spots. Her expertise in her field makes her fast at every task, and she constantly underestimates how long assignments take for others. She shows her disappointment when a task takes longer than she believed it should have. Jane is also decisive, almost never considering anyone else's input. Of course, Jane creates a fast-paced organization, and people have trouble keeping current. Her capability is beyond her team's capability. One-on-one, Jane is professional, warm, and thoughtful, but her blind spot for how an organization works eventually tears at the fabric of her personal relationships. When things get bad, Jane tries to fix the rift with ice-cream socials, pizza parties, bowling nights, and staff barbecues—a strategy she augments by spending more time at work herself, making the problems in the organization even worse.

As we did research into purposeful leadership, we analyzed more than 106,000 leaders' 360-degree feedback results. Three practices emerged as indicative of highly effective and purposeful leadership: building relationships, developing team members, and involving others.

Building Relationships

The single practice that emerged as highly correlated to our pattern of purposeful leadership was relationship building or networking. Purposeful leaders are known by many and know many other leaders. They are able to tap into wisdom and expertise from others quite easily. And their networking seems to know no bounds. In this regard, Priya is a standout. As she went through engineering school, she built networks. She frequents alumni events, often talks to undergraduates, maintains friendships with professors from her own alma mater and other engineering colleges around the world, and also manages to maintain a fairly large group of close friends. Nothing happens in the construction industry without her having a preview, if not an ability to influence it in some way. She is clearly guided by her personal vision and passion for building really cool projects, but she is also mastering the art of networking.

Developing Team Members

Just as effective in building engagement and commitment in an organization is developing the habit of creating experts and leaders behind you. This is quite the opposite of micromanaging. Leaders who grow leaders and functional experts build resilient organizations where people can choose to perform, choose to contribute, and choose to trust one another. Priya is again a standout in developing others. Many in the engineering world hold their roles as a direct result of her tutelage and mentorship. This is the next level of leadership, which includes a leader's responsibility to cultivate younger leaders, create succession and development plans, and involve younger leaders in strategic discussions.

In our framework of purposeful leadership, we would go so far as to say that leaders should have at least two successors they are developing, mentoring, and sponsoring. This is not idealistic thinking. It is common sense for leaders to understand they may not always be around but the organization will be, and the organization will need to have continuous, effective leadership. Many of our leadership experts and leadership development experts pointed out in their interviews while not every leader was great at developing talent, the best leaders were exceptional at building multiple successors. As one interviewee put it, "The best leader I ever worked with just had a knack for finding people that would actually be better in his job than he actually was, and he cultivated them during his tenure and gave them the self-confidence to take over any job and be themselves."

Involving Others

Yes, involving others in strategic discussions, opening up and finding people in the organization you normally wouldn't engage with, and talking about strategies and organizational health are all key aspects of purposeful leadership. There are many ways leaders can involve others. Just asking people for their opinion before you make a decision is a step in the right direction. This can take courage, emotional courage. It can also take wisdom and judgment to know how to reach beyond the "usual suspects" in an organization, the core group, and find people from different groups and points of view. It can take courage to listen to what they say, to listen for their insights on the organization, and to act on it. It also takes self-awareness to understand your biases and proclivities and to learn how to work past them and see people for who they are.

Priya is, again, a standout in her ability to involve others. Her education and career has helped her to embrace and celebrate talent. Her blind spot is around parts of the organization that don't have anything to do with engineering and construction per se.

Her impatience and her dismissal of finance, human resources, and most things technological have earned her a shadow reputation, one that she'll need to overcome as she moves ahead in her organization.

Scott Page, an economics professor at the University of Michigan, has quantified the value of inclusion, calling it the "diversity bonus." In his book *The Diversity Bonus*, he points out that the collective ability of a diverse team always beats the ability of a single individual, even if that individual has the highest IQ of the group. It takes a leader who willingly works with people in such a way as to find other perspectives that work or work even better. Diversity almost always exists.

Mastering inclusion or involvement has proved tough for many leaders. It is not something that you can force to happen as leaders grow and mature. And we cannot underestimate the organizational forces that sometimes create counter-messages around inclusive leadership. So what gets in the way? Our egos for one: our belief we have been appointed the leader because we have the answers, or our belief that we are the leader because we are *the expert*. Combine this with the games that sometimes get played in organizations that force us to think that, as leaders, we need to control every detail in our organizations, and you have a recipe for unintentional exclusion.

Of course, the same thing can result when leaders don't believe in their leadership ability. The lack of belief in one's own purpose, vision, and capability can create unworthiness and the need to attack the ideas of others. Leaders who don't believe in themselves can be even more problematic than leaders who dominate with their ego and their expertise. Regardless, followers disengage and feel excluded. New leaders who feel a need to prove themselves can often fall into this trap temporarily until they feel comfortable in their own skin in a new role or new organization.

Our research is compelling when you look at inclusion and inclusionary behaviors: inclusion is one of the strongest predictors of leadership effectiveness. We would love to say inclusion and engagement are the right thing to do, it is ethically correct, it is imperative for great problem solving, it accelerates innovation, and up and coming generations demand it. What we do say is that inclusion is critical to being effective as a leader. Effective, purposeful leaders find the experiences others have had and create the atmosphere that allows those perspectives to flourish and create great outcomes.

PURPOSE INSIDER

John Greven: Rhythm and Focus

John Greven, the founder of Greven Guitars, is quite accomplished in the guitar-making world. He's a Cornell University medical school grad who veered into his passion for woodworking and starting building and repairing guitars. He started at a famous guitar store in Nashville, then went on to lead the guitar-making function at Gibson and Martin before going out on his own. Here, he shares some fascinating ideas and insights on how leaders inspire people with their own flow and passion:

I deal with musicians, and when we talk about playing in the zone, it's a Zen experience. Everything is going really well, and they're in this space of channeling it as opposed to creating it. It's a peaceful and lovely place to be. It's the kind of thing you can achieve with any occupation. Neurosurgeons and even pilots have talked about it. Management could use this as a tool for resolving conflict and maintaining mental stability as they deal with daily affairs. Nevertheless, the zone is a hard place to get to. There is no roadmap to it. You have to work your way there. It comes as a surprise.

A way to get to that is being really focused, focused to the point where whatever space you are focused in is the world. You are it. It is you. You're not think-ing about anything or doing anything extraneous. The space triggers the mind into going to that special place. This can only benefit others. I've just "built guitars" every day for fifty years but, when building guitars, the relationship with people matters as much as or more than the actual wood or paint. Anytime you have more than one person in a relationship, you will have prob-lems. Being in the zone helps with those difficulties. It's how you listen, how you react, that often triggers neg-ative responses. If you listen from an engaging point of view and stay above the fray, in that zone, it is a much more effective way to communicate.

To be able to inspire, you usually have to be in the zone to figure something out that is worth being inspired about. We can teach people how to get there. To say you have the experience of that space and how you create that in the work environment—that is a challenge. But if you know what zone is and know you would like to be there more often, it is something worth practicing. Over time, when I was playing music or working on instruments, I would be in the zone more and more. It comes and goes. Because the work I do is so detailed and the fact I've been doing it forever, it is part of my autonomic nervous system at this point. I do what I do with such ease. If you want to name the zone, it's hyper attention.

Whether you are making music or anything else, focus draws you to that state. It goes back to that sense of Zen meditation where you lose yourself but you're still in the moment. I think we all need this. It would be a much better world if we could all get there . . . and often.

As a leader, we have to find that place where we are happy with ourselves, with what we are doing, and with whom we are doing it. Purposeful leadership is a relationship with ourselves and others. We all have to find what it looks like for us. What it feels like for us. What it is that we truly want to achieve as leaders. We have to find our reason, our purpose, for being a leader and then finding our zone for doing it.

PURPOSE INSIDER

Evolve to Full Team Engagement

She's been called "one of the most inspiring, engaging, high-achieving, and innovative humans to work with and for" by our respected staff members, so we don't take her insights lightly. "Team player" is an understatement when it comes to Melinda Babin, a longtime team builder and engagement strategist. She is an expert on team formation centered on personal why and organizational how. She explains:

> The world we live in is such a complicated, over-whelming place most of the time. A lot of people think about narrowing down what they are focused on and what will allow them to feel the most satisfaction from their job and benefits. I have conversations all the time that go along the lines of, "I want to understand what I am doing to impact people in a positive way and see my organization supporting this."
>
> This level of consciousness is totally empowered by other people along the way. You have to evolve to something that is larger than you. It's not just what you want and see but how you add to that collectively. Because of the way the world is today, a lot more people are looking for this connection. A lot of people need that. Some people struggle with finding what they are meant to do here and how they find like-minded people and like-minded organizations to align

themselves with and who will nurture that. People are searching for where they can grow and thrive to solve a bigger problem that will improve lives.

Much of my background is in advancement of tech and the balance between people engagement and inspiration. When I think about my own engagement, it is in two parts. The first is the organization itself. I'm a marketer. I help the organization find out who it is and share that with the world. Part of that is really understanding the impact that the organization has on the overall community. I'm doing consulting work with a company that does international operations. As I have walked around this organization and talked to people about why they do what they do, they don't tell me they help companies expand internationally, which is the company's tagline. What they say is, "We're helping companies work globally so everything they do aligns culture to culture and through different environments." It is a powerful statement. That part helps the company itself understand where it fits and what that purpose is. The second part is taking the vision of that purpose and applying it to the individual. Everyone understands the vision, and the role they are playing in that. I personally think the most powerful thing a manager does is understand what is of value to that individual person and if they are aligning that with their work. Once they are, they are so engaged and turned on about what it is they are doing that they're doing things you could not have dreamed up yourself.

Finally, if you're not leading purposefully, you're checking boxes. The real risk is that everything gets stagnant and stale. People become uninspired, unengaged. They leave and seek it somewhere else. I personally do not want to experience this. I left a role because of that. I was a marketer for an investment management software company. They needed to create a more modern marketing infrastructure. They had a team in place but no real leadership. They had a great product that was effective in the market. Initially I was excited. Then it became clear as I was working with that organization that they were not a purposeful organization. They were all about making money and not challenging status quo, not growing or innovating. It made me feel stuck in a creative crisis. I recognized this and moved on. What you end up with is an organization that is run by people that don't actually inspire or create innovation. What kind of culture do you have after this? Messy and disjointed. It is not a place that will attract PL [purposeful leadership]. That organization will die.

When I see Linkage's PL model of five commitments, it is something you have to embrace every day. It's not a process you go through. It's not an initiative. It's a way of thinking about something and nurturing it every day. It is a way of being.

More broadly, purposeful leadership is a holistic way of appreciating all the connections leaders need to make and how the commitments all flow through one thing: ourselves. We are the filter for everything that comes our way. We are the connection point of all interdependencies between the current state, our vision for the future, and all the people who engage with us to make it all happen.

THE NEW REALITY OF ENGAGEMENT

In the purposeful leadership model, engagement is much more than a flash of intimacy from leader to follower. It is the thread of intertwinement that sparks a sense of belonging and validation, ultimately propelling movement toward a goal. We asked a variety of leaders how they interpret engagement and its value among the commitments. We were not surprised by their seriousness; we were, in fact, thrilled by the range of positive interpretations and experiences centered in engagement.

Ann Schulte of Procter & Gamble said:

We have had a model at P&G with E's: Envision, Engage, Enable, Execute, and Empowerment. We got rid of every competency model. Leaders emphasize risk taking and urgency (we need to light a fire) while providing resources.

When I think of the engaging leader, I see my dad, reputed to be extremely high integrity, as everyone wanted to work for him. He was the No. 2 guy at Union Electric and yet he knew everyone's name—lunch lady, manager. We had so many people at his funeral. He was about relationships and recognizing others.

Valerie Norton of QBE Insurance stated:

Being there for people is engagement. Focus on behavior, not the person, the result and not the person. Be supportive of the human being. This creates trust. When there is trust, people will walk through walls for you. That is the key piece. They feel heard and supported. And even stretched. People say I "stretch" them and help them to believe in themselves. I have pushed them to new assignments in ways that you could not previously do. In engaging them, I want them to know I am here for them with an open mind. A leader I look up to is willing to be influenced. He is willing to be swayed and will give credit where credit is due. The leader I'm thinking of is a delight. He does not have to wordsmith every sentence. It is great for one's spirit for a leader to have confidence in you and it just makes life easier.

Anna Marie Kreitzman of Toyota, "where everyone is a leader with actual responsibilities to lead," said her boss is such a master of engagement that Kreitzman "wants to clone her." Kreitzman continued:

She is not that strategic. More tactical. Incredibly effective. Gets performance out of people who did not realize their capability. She brings out the best. She always ends up with a high-performing team. It is due to her leadership. Toyota is about problem-solving and continuous improvement, and as a result, can be negative and problem focused. Many of our leaders lead that way, but not her. She focuses on people's strengths. Her religious beliefs cause her to see the best in people and nurture that. She is able to correct and re-direct in a way that gives people some dignity. She embodies our principle for respect of people. This is not the US concept of respect; it is about challenge. Push you to your limits. Allow you to be the best you can be and nudging people to their best. It is demanding but also rewarding.

Taking a more philosophical approach to engagement, Richard Yeo of Singapore Post explains:

I'm a believer of someone needing to be a catalyst. You can't leave it to chance. Having a leader is a proactive way to getting greater success. The leader is there to make things happen and pull people together. It's like a multiplier. You put a multiplier on anything, the sum will be greater than its parts. Engage is interesting, because there are two schools of thought. One is a leader leads, and everybody follows.

The other is more decentralized. I like engage because I prefer the more "networked" type of leadership rather than the leader leading from the front. The value of the organization cannot hinge on the CEO. There must be a network of leaders so that the organization doesn't collapse when the leader leaves. It's just like having a table with 4 legs. Mobility of people is so high nowadays, and with the Millennial generation you don't expect people to stay forever. So in a network, when people leave, the network can reform itself. It's almost like our own body and how our cells regenerate. I've seen cases when a great leader leaves and the team disseminates, and that's such a waste. I've also seen cases where leaders actively involve others, even outside of their own area, in decision making. So there's a sense of joint accountability. Leaders need to be generous and confident enough to do this. This type of involvement helps to create sustainability in organizations. And you do need that in the new world.

Engagement is a function of the purposeful leader. The leader with a purpose who can symbolize and communicate that purpose is infectious. Particularly as the future gets uncertain and ambiguous, the purposeful leader symbolizes a clear path to a goal that provides people with a strong sense of where they are going and allows them to contribute to the journey.

The purposeful leader creates a collective of highly engaged people who all want the same goal and who work hard and collaborate together to achieve it. We cannot underestimate the value of leaders upping the game of their followers, and followers upping the game of their leaders.

PURPOSE INSIDER

Committed to Engage

Mary Beth Zick of Perrigo Co. makes the case that engagement and collaboration are intertwined. There is a mountain of evidence in our data that shows that she is correct in her thinking. Leaders work with shared vision not just personal vision. Shared vision provides a focal point for people to come together and work to create a future.

Zick comments:

What makes a leader exceptional at engaging others is collaboration. For example, our former chief scientist, now retired, had a scientist in each country. He brought them all face-to-face at least once a year. They mixed and mingled, and the team became stronger. He established a communication system. There was a schedule and cadence. It was thought out and given a timeline. That frequent and thoughtful communication fostered transparency in his organization. It was up and down as well as side-to-side communication. Also, caring, truly caring, about the people, not just the organization, really makes a difference. It's the human element. Are the leaders humble, team focused? Do they show they care through their policies? Their words and actions? How do they handle failure, especially in others? Do they know how to correct and then move on? Do they stay focused on the future and keep the human whole? Leaders focus on the issue, not the person. When you think about effectiveness, if you want people to follow you for purpose vs. compliance, you have to be worthy of the leadership responsibility.

ENGAGEMENT PROBE

- On the basis of your actions as a leader, are you contributing to the culture in a positive or negative way?

- Take an audit of your relationships. Whom are you close to? Whom do you trust? Who trusts you? With whom do you tend to have communication breakdowns? Whom do you hear from regularly? Whom don't you ever hear from?

- Does your vision for the organization speak to different generations? Different ethnicities? Different genders? Do people feel included in your vision?

- Do you have a shared vision? What would that feel like? What would that look like?

- Are you practiced in structuring teams in the right types of diversity? Are leaders who work for you or with you practiced in how to create a climate of inclusion? Are you?

- Have you gotten past the need to be in control? To be the expert? Can you honestly keep your ego in control?

- On the basis of your relationships today, in 10 years who will say that the person who most influenced them, developed them, and mentored their growth was you?

PART FOUR

INNOVATE

6

BANISH THE STATUS QUO AND BREAK THROUGH

Imagination is more important than knowledge.

—*Albert Einstein, theoretical physicist*

> ## COMMITMENT: INNOVATE
>
> *Drive new thinking and creative freedom*
> *and reimagine realities for*
> *competitive differentiation and success.*

New Yorker magazine wrote a review on the movie *The Post*. The movie tells the story of how Katharine Graham goes from being a widow to owner of the *Washington Post* to amazing leader, finding her voice. Here we have an individual who was not initially a leader and through circumstances assumes a leadership role, finds her purpose, and starts to manifest her leadership in a positive way. I was stunned at what a great story it is about a person learning to lead in a nontraditional manner. Where is the training? Where is the time spent in the newsroom learning to write? Where is the time spent editing? What about her ability to sell advertising? In a metaphorical way, it's almost as if Katharine Graham had invented her leadership in a garage and disrupted an industry in leading without learning how to lead.

Many of our beliefs about innovation start with some story about two people in a garage.

In our research into purposeful leadership, we found innovation to be one of the hardest of the commitments for leaders to master, with less than a fourth of leaders consistently demonstrating the behaviors that drive innovation. Before we go any further, we need to say that the primary outcome of quality leadership is *change*. Leaders create change. If you are currently leading an organization that is basically the same as it was two years ago, then you have not really led.

INNOVATION AND LEADERSHIP

Innovation does what almost nothing else can: It keeps a company competitive. There are so many ways a culture and its leadership can stifle innovation that innovation remains an elusive game.

Innovation creates a domino effect of multiple changes both inside the organization and outside the organization. Scanning the world, the economy, your industry, and your competitors is paramount. Truly empathizing with and understanding your customers is just as critical, if not more so. Networking with a broad array of different stakeholders who can test and improve your ideas is challenging and difficult but essential. Developing an inspiring goal for innovation is perhaps the differentiator.

Teacher and mentor Donella Meadows used to say, "Great goals change everything." Truly, there are so many different ways to read those four words! One subtle way to read that statement is, "Great goals spark innovation in your organization." While our 360-degree results on leaders have innovation as the lowest-scoring commitment, the interviews we did with experts gave us a different and better understanding of what this truly means.

Several experts we interviewed reflected the better leaders they have seen operate firsthand have been extremely good at figuring out where innovation needs to happen, even if they haven't a clue about what innovation needs to take place. As one expert described it:

> We were losing our competitiveness as a company, and we were perplexed. We looked at hundreds of presentations on the issue, we benchmarked every similar organization, we surveyed customers multiple times. But no answer.
>
> Our CEO then went out and literally sat outside our stores and just watched what happened. Multiple stores, multiple locations. He came into an executive team meeting one morning and announced that we needed to change our point of sale (POS) system. Of course, he also said he knew nothing about POS systems. He challenged the team to figure out how he might be wrong.
>
> But in the end after collecting more data all they did was end up proving him right.
>
> In every previous attempt to find the problem we had never considered the POS. We ended up buying a

new POS system that helped us manage our store inventory, and move the customer through the sale faster. We regained our competitiveness almost within a quarter of having it fully operational.

To put it simply, the purposeful leader is exceptional at targeting where innovation needs to occur: the POS, the culture, the product or service, the messaging, the warranty. Whether or not purposeful leaders are innovative or creative themselves is unimportant; they understand and are able to set goals around the right place to spark innovation.

INNOVATING NAVIGATION

Retired Jeppesen CEO Mark Van Tine had long been guided by a personal why of making aviation safer, simpler, and more cost-effective for a million pilots worldwide. But his leadership path didn't start in the friendly skies.

Although the airline industry is one of the safest and most regulated in the world, a tragic accident in 1995—American Airlines Flight 965—changed everything, according to Van Tine. And that accident, combined with Van Tine's why of safety aviation, sparked an innovation that improved airline safety by increasing a pilot's situational awareness and reducing the pilot's workload.

"My company did not do anything wrong," said Van Tine. He explained:

But I consider it representative of what we did as an industry. It was an industry accident. The complexity of the technology diverted the pilots' attention from the simple

fact that the plane was continuing to descend in mountain-
ous terrain. When the pilots finally figured out what they
needed to do, their situational awareness was so depleted
that the plane ran into a mountain. This influenced me to
stay focused on the information provided to the pilots and
how it was used in the cockpit. Accessing the information
had become so complicated that it increased pilot workload and created confusion.

We [Jeppesen] needed to take a strong leadership
role in how information is used in the cockpit. We digi-
tized this information in 1996 for use in standard com-
puters, but we didn't have a simple device in the airplane
to display it. You couldn't bring a laptop on board because
of regulations. We had a strong brand, but we were still
viewed as a stodgy 75-year-old company, so we had to
change our reputation in the industry.

In 2003, we created the business case for change—
how to get millions of pages of paper aviation maps into a
usable form and display it in a digital form. In 2010, Apple
introduced the iPad to the world. By 2018, the world was
flying with tablets, and our digital maps were a big part of
that. We had to get our old paper infrastructure converted
to digital form. And because we started early, we were
ready when the iPad came out.

The company faced common business challenges at the time:
to remain relevant to customers and to avoid being commod-
itized by advancing technology. Working on Jeppesen's overall
leadership effectiveness, Van Tine set an organizational vision:
*Make Jeppesen the most essential element in a pilot's informa-
tion toolbox.* The objective was to "make the complex simple" for

Jeppesen's customers and reduce the pilot's workload in the cockpit. The company focused on redefining its goals, reshaping the team made up of the top 100 leaders at Jeppesen, and revising its operational priorities to reflect a participative model for innovation. Plus, the leaders placed a laser focus on transforming the company from a paper-based business model into a digital information enterprise.

The company secured more than 100 new patents, and Jeppesen's annual revenue grew from $260 million in 2002 to roughly $1 billion in 2015.

How do you arrive an innovation? Sometimes the events are catastrophic. The tragedy of American Airlines Flight 965 was incredible; lives were lost. Should the accident have been prevented? Of course it should have. "We didn't do anything wrong, but we didn't do everything we could. That was a galvanizing moment." It created a strong sense of how Mark could live his purpose and lead his organization with an inspiring direction, collective engagement, and innovation that would save lives.

THREE PATHS TO LEADERSHIP INNOVATION

In this regard, *James* is our mathematical innovator, a real challenger. His command of his business is so good he constantly discovers discrepancies and inconsistencies. He finds something in the numbers that leads him to a challenging question and a new way of thinking about how and what he and his colleagues put into the marketing messages as a company. When he first started to find irregularities in the data, his colleagues would groan and roll their eyes. They were not thrilled with his challenges to their "wisdom." James needed hours of individual meetings with each of them to make an advance in changing the way that they would see the world. They gradually came to see, time after time, that he had "something." And it took a while for them, as peers, to stop seeing James's challenges as good or bad and for them to stop withdrawing or criticizing every time he found a new irregularity to take advantage of and innovate.

Not surprisingly, based on everything we have disclosed, *Priya* is the most innovative. She simply exposes herself to everything and everyone in engineering and design and develops a gut instinct about what is happening. She is high risk and high reward. Her talented staff never sputters or hesitates around her hunches, and she and her staff find the architects that reflect the more interesting design concepts that Priya inspirationally paints with her impassioned speeches during project meetings. Unfortunately, when her twists and turns impact the rest of her organization, the complexity slows things down, and Priya is often at a loss for answers. She sees herself as customer focused and doesn't understand why the organization doesn't immediately respond to her changes.

If she is promoted within the organization, she will need to learn how to coordinate and integrate every function of the organization together to begin to achieve overall organizational excellence through innovation.

Jane, in innovating, is perhaps the most symbolic of what we found in our research about purposeful leaders: She is uncanny in her ability to target the right thing in the organization, then set the right goal to innovate, and have it pay off.

On the surface Jane seems to show a preference for things to be the same. She seems to like consistency, order, structure, and familiarity. Her nondescript call center is quite large; the building in which it is housed is the size of multiple football fields. You would be hard-pressed to figure out what company she works for simply by walking through the center. Her office is not where you'd expect; it's not in the corner. She converted the corner office into a large conference room. She sits in the center on the far left side of the building. She has to walk the entire length of the center each morning and each night to enter or leave the building. Her direct reports flank her down the long side of the building.

Jane involves herself in too many decisions in the call center. Her day is packed with meetings, most of which occur in her conference room. Her direct reports describe her as constantly in evaluation mode. The center collects hundreds of metrics, and Jane reviews them daily, like television executives review the overnight audience numbers on their shows. She assigns not just the good-bad evaluation but also the strong-weak correlation to things. In other words, some things are bad, but they have a weak or meaningless impact on customers. Some things are bad and have a strong impact on customers. Some activities have no impact at all, and she wonders why they even do them.

In day after day of these types of meetings, her direct reports develop action plans, and Jane waits to see the result in the metrics. She is constantly looking for the decision that will create the most positive impact while reducing the number of negative outcomes. When she repeatedly sees areas where actions have no positive or negative impact, she starts to look for some way to change the goal, shake things up. In some cases, she starts to see patterns between metrics and starts thinking about what could be different.

Jane is constantly toying with her call center policies, rules, and even sometimes people's mindsets to find an improvement in her organization's results. She is relentless in finding a meaningful gap in how things get done and its impact on customers. She and her team find solutions and test them. If there is no change in the measured outcomes, they test new solutions. She can be intensely vigilant in trying to find a real working solution.

Jane's status as a high performer in her organization is built on multiple technology and software implementations that have not only created improved performance but also created steep improvements in the metrics. She's compulsive in her daily evaluations, but it takes a lot to motivate her to change something in the way the organization operates.

As one of her direct reports said, however, "Watch out when she decides to make a change, because it wholesale changes everything." And as one of her peers put it:

> Jane doesn't always see and understand every impact her new goals have on other functions and departments that support her, and we often end up getting in trouble with our superiors for busting our budgets and drifting off our functional goals. But something about what she does and how she functions, she gets amazing results. So everyone gives her a pass and joins in. In the end she figures out how much we had to bend in order to help her, and she is always grateful.

MASTERING INNOVATION

In looking at leaders in our research, we found three primary innovation practices:

- Exploring and navigating opportunities
- Changing the game
- Leading change

Explore and Navigate Opportunities

We heard a multiplicity of themes about effective leaders relative to innovation and change. Leadership experts and leadership development experts alike identified several key behavioral patterns around innovation. First, the innovative leaders were externally focused. We heard estimates that these leaders spent as much as 80 percent of their time on external issues, customer engagement, economics, and competition. Second, they tended to see the world as full of opportunities, and they just had to find the right ones. Third, they tended to focus conversations and meetings on what could be done and not on what had already happened.

As Warren Bennis pointed out so many years ago in *On Becoming a Leader*, they encouraged dissent. They "tested and measured."

Change the Game

What Warren Bennis called "tests and measures," we might call action learning today, that is, constantly testing new ideas and new ways of putting the organization together to create new ideas for running the business and for introducing new products or services. Following the rule of keeping what works and discarding what doesn't keeps the organization in a constant state of learning and change. Other leaders take more sophisticated approaches by trying to find ways to change the operating system of a market, an organization, or a customer type. When you change the operating system, you are really transforming what is happening in a given environment. This requires that you change not just how something happens, but the rules or policies governing how it happens. It takes a real eye for detail to lead change this way.

Lead Change

Leading is, essentially, leading change. There is a drumbeat of change happening outside an organization. Asymmetries in natural resources, demographics, technology, governance, and globalization drive that change. You can hunker down and ignore it, or you can figure it out as best you can despite the complexity, the dilemmas, and the uncertainty of it all. You can test and measure your best thinking.

There is never a time when the world is not changing. Your role as a leader is to lead (not manage) change in your systems, processes, and people to stay ahead of the changes that are negatively impacting your success as an organization. Yes, there will be resistance to change because negative energy always seems to have a more dominant impact on people than positive energy. You have to be more communicative more often regarding the vision and the goals. As the leader, you have to not just own the vision; you must also own the drumbeat and sense of urgency around the change. You must always be the role model for the change. You must master the use of symbols in how you act, how you communicate, and how you highlight people in meetings, town halls, and other events. Despite the need for control you may have, you have to let go and include others. Despite everything that your intuition tells you, you must become a truth teller. Master the pattern of inspiring truth telling that other master communicators and leaders have patterned:

- Describe the situation truthfully and briefly.

- Explain your solution and its purpose enthusiastically.

- Highlight three to five motivating points showing why the solution will work.

- Be honest about the challenges of implementation.

- Express your belief in success because of the people who will be involved.

- Eliminate the games that people can and do play during change.

It's normal human behavior to be self-protective, to try to gain advantage for oneself, and to lose perspective. As a positive, purposeful leader, you can call out the behaviors and erase their effectiveness. Mastering change is tantamount to mastering leadership. Leading is creating change.

PURPOSE INSIDER

Burst of Innovation

Burst, founded by purposeful entrepreneur Bryant McBride, enables broadcasters, media companies, rights holders, and brands to instantly deliver mobile video to broadcast, OTT, digital, and social platforms at low cost. Burst's technology allows reporters, viewers, fans—anyone with a smartphone, a point of view, and a subject to record—to get their video into live or curated media streams seamlessly without requiring the download and use of a mobile app to participate. For media companies, live event venues, brands, and marketers, this means fresh and compelling content that is rights-controlled and readily monetized with no workflow disruption.

McBride has spearheaded seven companies, cementing his dedication to innovation early in life, with sports and technology coming together in a variety of ways to delight masses. McBride explains:

> Part of the approach to innovation has to be an urgency that pervades from the top to the bottom. A lot of people talk a good game about it, but do they behave like their livelihoods depend on it? Mission-critical: you have to get this done or go out of business. Innovation requires constantly re-examining, reinventing, and rethinking. This is the core. An extreme example of this that completely blows me away is Steve Jobs. He figured out how to save Apple with the iPod. If you're not growing, you're dying. To infuse the need for innovation at every level of the organization is hard. Innovation brings purpose that people feel they are on a mission. The money is the byproduct.
>
> At Burst, what we are trying to do every day is keep people focused on the mission. What fuels us is the ability to use user-generated content in positive ways that benefit lots of people, cementing the relationship between media and consumers. People can be part of a conversation that helps others. I do my best to make sure that everyone I work with feels excited to come to work, that work isn't just full of essential tasks but instead that there is a special experience to be involved in and that people are learning

and growing, that they are rewarded for their contribution, and that they are given constructive feedback
to make it better. As a leader committed to innovate,
that is my primary job.

Mcbride sees the connection between innovation, inspiration,
engagement, and achievement, his role, and his leadership journey.
He understands how his leadership plays out in his simple articula-
tion of what causes what when leading.

PURPOSE INSIDER

Hackensack Meridian Health:
A Culture of Well-Being and Purpose

What kind of organization do you get when you combine
two experienced companies with different cultures? Can
the ultimate organizational purpose bring it all together?
Hackensack Meridian has fused a variety of innovation
methodologies together and has actually started to do
an organizational restructure that will further transform
the organization and provide substantial opportunities
for high-performing individuals to advance their careers.
The company has also begun a journey of transforming
numerous cultures across the organization into one culture. The mission is to transform healthcare and to be recognized as the leader of positive change. The vision is that
innovation is part of its DNA. In addition, the company

created and communicated four beliefs as the basis for the behaviors that support these lofty goals.

Here, Patrice Ventura, vice president of Talent Development & Organizational Effectiveness, and Nancy Corcoran-Davidoff, chief experience officer, share how they did it.

To begin, Ventura says:

> Leadership is a responsibility. We always tell our leaders through everything we do that they are the most important person to their team. Things can be going on in the organization, but how does that leader communicate what is going on and interact with the team and support the team to reach their potential? If a person would like to develop herself and practice and if she has self-awareness, she can lead purposefully. People have to want it, and people can transform. No one can help them to do that. A coach can assist the thinking process, but the person has to want to do it.
>
> What's so great about Hackensack Meridian Health is that our mission is purposeful. We're health care. What I see our leaders working hard to do— especially as they move up in the organization—is not to lose touch with the front line. We have 33,000 employees and growing. We're here to take care of patients and loved ones, so it's not just the patient who comes into the hospital. It's their family and friends. We have to take care of that whole system.
>
> In our culture, we have the four C's: Compassionate, Courageous, Creative, and

Collaborative. We decided to design our team member behaviors or attributes and our leader behaviors related to the four C's. We provide detailed definitions so people can have conversations throughout the year about how people are doing, but we are a leader in how to deliver health care in an innovative way. We have the full continuum of care: hospitals, physician offices, nursing homes, ambulatory care, rehabs, integrative health. We try to connect the dots so when people come in, they have a network of care to receive. It's about keeping people healthy. We call it the continuum of care.

When you look at the purposeful leadership commitments, how we are hiring is changing, how we train people is changing. We have to think differently even from a development standpoint. Should it just be classroom? Definitely not. It should be experience also. That is how people learn. We have mentoring and coaching opportunities within our 16 hospitals and all the other facilities. In some industries, people may go through the motions, but in health care you need people present and engaged. As a leader, you need to look at how your team is functioning and how they are communicating. If they aren't helping each other so that no one fails, there will be a problem somewhere. We're on a journey to becoming a high-reliability organization. We have a lot of development opportunities around how to apply design thinking and high-reliability strategies and techniques. This expands into how to be a leader in other areas. At the core, it comes from within you. That is the *become*. Different challenges arise and the world changes. You need to adjust, but you need to hold onto your core values and flex your skills in different ways. You have to be not only introspective about yourself as a leader and contributor, you also need to see how the world is changing and how to adjust.

Corcoran-Davidoff adds:

To bring that back to leadership, we believe the leaders in our organization need different skills to be successful. For example, when you are an organization focused on innovation and transformation, leaders have to be extremely agile. They need to be able to adjust course and work at a fast pace. Because of this path we are pursuing, we're being contacted by a lot of potential partners. Sometimes it feels there is so much going on, but in this environment leaders need to understand that these opportunities may not come around again. Or if they do, competitors may step into them first. Agility is critical.

Innovation at all levels is encouraged. We're creating an environment where we can invest in products that we believe will transform health care. In that vein, we created our version of the Shark Tank, where we committed a substantial amount of money. People are pitching their ideas. Bringing all these things together—new skills for leaders emphasizing agility and innovation, an environment that supports those new skills, inspirational leadership—this is our focus. Our culture allows people to evolve, to become.

Hackensack Meridian Health is a developmentally focused organization. People are always becoming, and the organization is constantly evolving and innovating as a result. The richness and complexity of all this activity has a simple outcome: better care, better caretakers, and better organization.

MANY PATHS TO INNOVATION

Bryant McBride and Mark Van Tine, whom we introduced earlier in the chapter, were indeed on the cutting edge of organizations that both supported and necessitated innovation. But technology is not the sole breeding ground for leaders who push for innovation.

Lisa Donovan of Sage Hospitality offers:

We have an innovative leader on the executive team now. The mantra is, "Do different stuff, like put a restaurant with a bee hive on top of a high rise." They created a garden and a bee hive on top of a LEED Gold-certified building alongside a restaurant. The bees are used for products that go to the spa. The greens end up in the salad.

When I think of Sage Hospitality, I also think of CEO Walter Isenberg ("One-Minute Walter"). He needs just one minute to get on stage and to get inspirational. He does it on a dime. We spent a year innovating our purpose statement. The new statement is, "Enriching lives one minute at a time." Think of customers—take a minute to make their experience better; owners—what can we do that will enrich their value; employees—what can we do with a minute to help them: skills enrichment. Walter drove the work. He sees the value of the pithy vision. I know some of the facts of his life that make him care about these things. His parents were concentration camp survivors. He has a strong sense of right and wrong. When the underdog is kicked, he goes into overdrive to care for people. He makes it a point to go into the employee cafeteria, gets our old mac and cheese, and sits down with the people. He remembers people and asks about family. This is a demanding industry; this is a 24/7 fast industry. People tend to work themselves to death. Housekeepers have to turn sixteen rooms in an eight-hour shift. They need that inspiration. That the CEO would sit and ask about family makes all the difference.

Maura Stevenson of Wendy's explains:

There has been a false dichotomy between management and leadership, and I'm glad to see the balance here with purposeful leadership. I think this is missed. Purposeful leadership has multiple pairs of tensions: inspire and achieve; innovate and engage; innovate and achieve; inspire and innovate. Inspiring without achievement is not success—we want new ideas that are executable. There are tensions among all the commitments. When you resolve these tensions, you reach become, and then you are in a position to help people get what they need to reach to their next level.

There are a number of ways to be innovative that don't necessarily require creativity. Innovation can occur virtually anywhere in an organization, such as packaging or even a succession plan. At Wendy's, we got our entire succession process to a one page tool. There are lots of different ways to be innovative, and you should always be looking at ways to innovate everywhere. Be careful not to limit people. I'm not creative, but my 360 considers me innovative, a change leader. I stay new and innovative. The capability to be outstanding at innovation is somewhat dependent on your internal wiring. Also, how are people encouraged to think about problems? Are they encouraged to explore? Are they naturally curious? Intrigued by ideas? And at some level are they constantly dissatisfied? Do they have a fear of complacency? Just look at how education has changed. No longer memorization but rather applying and connecting dots, expressing a breadth and curiosity about things.

Finally, though banking is still thought of as a traditional industry despite the online bells and whistles and instant cash drops, Jamal Bakri of RHB Bank leads and observes innovation every day. He says:

Leaders exist to make a positive difference to the organizations they work in and the world they operate in.

A good leader will provide direction, innovation, and impact beyond business results. For example, in the world he or she leads, the leader must build a sense of community, build future leaders, and be able to change the way people do things in a positive way.

When they look at innovation, a true leader needs to look at the hiring of people as well. There must be a focus on attitude, disposition, and perspectives rather than just their CV and experiences. The environment must also allow for diversity to encourage innovation. The five commitments of purposeful leadership are easy for me to remember. Our current leadership competency model is too complicated and hard to remember. Simple is beautiful.

The beauty of innovation is that there is not just one way of doing it. That doesn't mean that there aren't methods and processes to help us innovate or that we should give up trying to create a "code" for innovating. Innovation helps us to achieve our inspiring goals. The leader's role is to target where the competitive innovation needs to happen. The leader must also listen for other innovations that happen in his or her team or function and not be too restrictive. It is a leader's responsibility to deepen everyone's appreciation for the role that innovation can play in an organization.

For Linkage, leadership is about this "becoming," where you are forming a character, your ethics, and your purpose. You are self-aware and have a conviction. For the past 30 years, leadership development has focused on a distinct set of competencies (see the sidebar "Leadership Competencies") and has largely gotten away from leadership as the formation of character, integrity, responsibility and respect for others, trustworthiness, and ethics. As we have seen, we are not getting better at developing leaders. What was fascinating in our exemplars is where effective leaders show up and lead with no training, no development, no time on task, similar to Katharine Graham at the *Washington Post.* However, they do show up as purposeful, engaging, innovative leaders with a capacity to adapt and learn.

In some decision-making systems, you often try to find the decision that is going to create the most positive outcomes while reducing the number of negative outcomes. If you look at statistics from Gallup, only 2 in 10 leaders—and this means up to a CEO managing people—build the mastery to lead. About 6 in 10 are good enough and still learning albeit probably too slowly or learning the wrong things, and about 2 in 10 are damaging to the culture, the people, and the business. Our analysis of our purposeful leadership assessment data is similar. Using the decision-making system as a metaphor, leadership development systems should be measuring which leaders are producing positive outcomes and figuring out how that happened in order to do more of it. Continuing with the metaphor, leadership development systems should be measuring which leaders are producing negative outcomes and eliminating those leaders who cannot be salvaged with an improvement plan. We need to reinvent how we do leadership development.

INNOVATION PROBE

- How often do you think about "nothing"?

- How often do you scan the outside world for trends and patterns relevant to your organization?

- What sources or types of information do you regularly or routinely overlook or dismiss?

- When it comes to the world beyond your organization's doors, what are your three blind spots?

- Have you ever been blindsided by an internal or an external innovation?

- How do you handle a consequential decision (a decision you cannot take back or reverse)? As if it's life or death, or "one step at a time"?

- If your competition were really astute, how would it defeat you in the marketplace?

- What culture and attitude do you need to cultivate for your team to be innovative?

- Let's imagine that the next year is actually four semesters of graduate school for you. What will you learn about in the first semester, the second, the third, and the fourth? What will you do with what you've learned?

- What one innovation would make a significant impact on your leadership outcomes? How would you write a goal for that one thing?

7

THE TECHNICAL VERSUS THE LEADERSHIP DILEMMA

Leadership is the art of giving people a platform for spreading ideas that work.

—*Seth Godin, former dot-com executive and author*

In the summer of 1972, the world sat transfixed and entertained by, of all things, the World Chess Championship between defending champion Boris Spassky of the then Soviet Union and his U.S. challenger, Bobby Fischer. It was sports, politics, theater, and weirdness all at the same time.

Decades later, I was seated beside a man named James Slater on a commercial flight from London to the United States. At the time, I was a young supervisor in the financial services industry, and I did not much like the role of supervisor compared with the more technical role of underwriter.

Mr. Slater explained to me that in every industry there are various perspectives that one can take, and using the chess championship as an example, he explained those levels. First, obviously, there are the chess combatants, the players. This is where the fame and glory reside, he said. But there is also the referee, especially for the world championships, which is an honored role to be chosen for and to fulfill: keeping the game fair for both sides. Then there is FIDE, which is the World Chess Federation governing body that oversees the world rating system as well as the world title and other titles, publishes and manages the rules of the game, maintains membership, develops fund-raising, and promotes the game. FIDE's role also encompasses a great deal of fame and glory, but it's a much more expansive context. A chess match also needs someone to promote the match, publicize and advertise the match, and do site management and vendor management. Each of these roles requires unique expertise and has a unique role to play in the World Chess Championship.

Mr Slater exhorted me to find the level that I was good at and play at that level. He was an accountant but found that he had other more valuable skills that built on those accounting skills. This gave him the opportunity to become a business manager for events, a role he really loved. He started with small events to build his skills, graduated to national events to build his reputation, and relearned everything to jump into grand scale international events. At each level he kept focusing on the capacity and capability of his team to deal with the various issues different events attract. He encouraged me to find the level in the insurance industry where I might play best. I might be a great underwriter, but I might be even better managing the underwriting process, or leading a financial services business, or working for the industry, or maybe working as a regulator. Every role has different skills, different interests, and a different risk profile for the individual. He couldn't think of an industry that didn't have this kind of array of roles and responsibilities. If I wanted to stay with a single company, then there were different roles with different skill sets, interests, and risk profiles as well that I should be exploring, and each also has a different scale: individual contributor, team leader, functional leader, business leader, enterprise leader.

The Center for Creative Leadership has documented the way leaders scale in terms of size of operation. We were more interested in how they formed their identity as a leader.

In other words, there is no dilemma between soft skills and hard skills, between technical skills and leadership skills. It is a fake dichotomy. Each perspective or role requires certain organizing skills and certain technical skills. Each role has different complexities and different risks to manage. Of course, each position has different exposure or visibility, which creates its own set of risks. Not everyone wants the responsibility for making decisions for other people. Not everyone feels comfortable being responsible for the work and the decisions of other people.

In doing our research, we found that the leaders we interviewed were admittedly ambitious, though not ambitious in the sense of personal gain. They each wanted to make their mark, accomplish something bigger than themselves, make a difference in the world. Some were business majors, others were engineers, some studied security, and some just followed their childhood passions. We interviewed a college president, a chief of police for a large city, a nuclear power plant manager, a president of a railroad, a hospital administrator, a superintendent of schools, a head of a company that provided dietitian services, video game designers, an executive who led a company that designed amusement park rides, and a leader of a company that taught extreme driving skills to wannabe race-car drivers.

About 35 percent of our sample were liberal arts majors with no clear idea about what industry they wanted to enter or what company they wanted to work for after graduation, but they did have clear ideas about what they did not want to do. To a person, they all loved what they did every day and wanted to do something with it that was meaningful, purposeful. None of them admitted to thinking at the start that one day they would be "leaders" of large organizations. They all reveled in the technical aspects of their chosen careers. In the cases of our three high potentials: James went to college and majored in marketing, Priya majored in civil engineering, and Jane was a liberal arts major with no clear idea of what she wanted after college. We did find among all our leaders some clear ideas of how their perspective and their role changed as they worked to do something "bigger than themselves."

Several dominant themes emerged among the leaders we interviewed concerning how they found their personal and professional purpose. For each of the leaders we talked with and researched, their identity as a leader formed around multiple themes.

WIDEN YOUR FOCUS

Regardless of whom we talked to, every leader reflected on the value of always seeking a wider perspective. For example, if you are an engineer who builds or constructs houses, then widen your perspective to what's happening in marketing, sales, warranty, and finance. Then widen your perspective again and look around at your industry and your competition. Next, look at what's happening with housing in general: in your community, your state, the country. After that, try to figure out what's going on culturally with housing: trends, issues, and opportunities. Keep pulling the lens back and include more and more diverse perspectives, more and different types of problems that are part of the dynamic of your industry, and more ways to explain what's actually happening.

For all our leaders that we interviewed, nothing was as valuable as their practice of "widening their lens." Multiple leaders advocated for reading widely and often.

HAVE A PERSONAL PASSION

All our leaders, as their practice of widening their lens became more useful, said they developed a passion for a particular issue or set of issues in their industry. For more than one individual, safety was a particular passion. For other individuals, their energy, excitement, and enthusiasm came from helping others.

All the leaders we interviewed said their passion was directly responsible for what would ultimately become their leadership vision. The things they found deeply and personally meaningful in their industry ultimately became what not only inspired them but also was contagious enough to inspire others. For each of them, they also were able to see different periods when their passion lagged, and they saw the engagement and passion of their stakeholders wane as well. For most of the leaders, this resulted in a big "aha" moment: I need more leaders than just myself energizing this organization. They realized they needed to build a network of leaders with a passion for the vision.

DON'T JUST LIVE YOUR VALUES— ENLARGE THEM

Many of our leaders discussed their values as the core of what they became as leaders, not values in name only, but in action. The leaders we interviewed talked about finding a way to scale their values in their industry. For instance, one leader was very much the scientist as a child and as a student. He entered the workforce after school in an industry that was still largely based on intuition, preferences, and tradition. Because of this, for a long time he felt a bit trapped and really hated the industry. However, he gradually came to see his "geek's eye for data" was not only something he valued but something that could add value. He ended up building a company and transforming an industry around his love of data.

DON'T IGNORE THE OBVIOUS

Notice what you see.

The leaders we researched and talked to all made reference to a common phenomenon that was so obvious we almost overlooked it: Pay attention to what you see. Passions can be blinding in multiple ways. For example, years ago I was an executive coach to a leader who ran the entire western region of his company. Even though his company sold a range of products, he had grown up in one division of the company and had a strong passion for the value and benefits of the products from his original division. He carried this passion over into many other areas, often citing the division as the model organization to the other divisions, promoting mostly from that division, favoring investments in that division, and providing extra perks to key talent in that division. Everyone else felt disengaged, disempowered, and excluded. He couldn't see his own behavior was creating a "success to the successful" pattern in his territory. Look carefully at everything and everyone. Find the patterns. Sometimes the leaders we talked to said, "Not only is the thing you need to see right in front of you, but thousands of people have completely overlooked it."

GET COMFORTABLE
WITH YOUR JUDGMENT

Most of the leaders we talked to reflected on the discomfort they felt making decisions on behalf of others. As one leader put it: "Leadership isn't just about accomplishing something bigger than yourself; it's also about caring for and making decisions on behalf of some pretty large groups of people. And even when they are with you, they don't always agree with every decision you make. It took me years to make my peace with that."

It's important that you be able to find and work with the data you need as your leadership scales. In larger organizations politics can obscure what leaders need to see to make good judgments.

VALUE AND EMPATHIZE
WITH YOUR CUSTOMERS

One leader we talked to had a secret formula for making decisions and figuring out strategies and next steps. He simply kept asking one question: "Is what we are doing what's best for our customers?" The secret is not such a great secret, of course. Aspiring to make a difference in the lives of your customers has been a key ingredient of business for decades, but it's surprisingly absent in a great many businesses these days. Empathy can come in many forms, for example, making your product or service more affordable or more available or safer or of higher quality.

One leader we interviewed spent his entire career learning how to better manage inventory so that customers could buy what they needed when they needed it. When the CEO role came open and the organization needed to manage multiple different acquisitions and brands in one integrated inventory at more than 800 locations, he was the one who could create the goal and manage the organization of it. Another leader we worked with created a more affordable line of the company's flagship products. This leader told us, "I kept hearing from customers who couldn't afford our product. They were working musicians and younger than our standard customers without the same kind of disposable income. It meant finding ways to save on labor and material, and more importantly, it meant finding a new distribution system, but we can now look at having these customers for a lifetime."

BE A BEGINNER—
HAVE A BEGINNER'S MIND

One leader we talked to reminded us that the root of the word "innovation" comes from the word meaning "novice." A leader must truly delve into any issue with a beginner's mind. Even when you think you have mastery over an area, it may have been some time since you worked in that area, and things could have changed substantially over time. "You need real patience and doggedness sometimes to figure out things that you actually think you know. I can rebuild a carburetor in a car, but cars haven't had them in decades," relayed another leader.

FOCUS YOUR ACTIONS

We heard lots of differing opinions from our interviewees on focus. Some said to find the vital few issues and concentrate on those, while others said to focus on whatever you decide you are going to do. Either way, the idea our leaders tried to communicate is "Do whatever you are going to do with intensity." The caution that leaders expressed was "Make sure you aren't 'peanut-buttering' your intensity and commitment." You cannot do everything and solve every problem, so don't try. Make a big difference in everything you do rather than make small differences in lots of things. As they say, "Less is more."

ELIMINATE BLIND SPOTS AND WEAKNESSES

An important thought that our research turned up was the basic idea a leader must constantly work to eliminate blind spots or weaknesses. While knowing and having superpowers is great, leadership is a lifelong journey requiring constant fine tuning of a leader's capabilities. As the world keeps changing and our organizations keep changing, leadership capability cannot remain stagnant. As leaders scale up an organization, they will develop new blind spots as a result of the scale and scope of change. Leaders need to find their current blind spots and eliminate them.

BE ETHICAL

It may be the times that we live in, but 100 percent of the leaders we interviewed talked about ethics as a source of growth. In fact, most leaders we talked to expressed surprise at just how much there was to learn about the ethics of their businesses and organizations. "I came up through customer service roles as I was learning how to lead, and I thought I had ethics mastered. But once I got into enter-prise roles, I had to learn about the ethics of the research we were doing. I also had to learn about the ethics of dealing with regula-tors, the ethics of banking, and the ethics of being part of a commu-nity and a state," mused one leader.

APPRECIATE AND HONOR THE PAST

A surprising theme about leadership growth came up when lead-ers talked about "taking a guided tour of your organization's past." Leaders must understand and acknowledge they are building on past generations. "It's easy to sit and criticize," reflected one leader, "but at some point you have to recognize people always do the best that they can for where they are in time. You can't call every deci-sion in the past a bad decision. It doesn't do you any good as a leader to criticize everyone and everything." Learn to honor the people and the accomplishments of the past while using your scholarship to build a future. "What's done is done," said one leader. "If it was amazing, it's done. If it didn't work, it's done. Find what still reso-nates about the past, honor it, and rock and roll into the future."

DON'T REST ON YOUR LAURELS

The leaders we interviewed collectively expressed probably the sin-gle most important theme about leadership growth: If you sit on your accomplishments, you are guaranteed not to see any new ones.

"When I first broke into enterprise leadership, I was about forty-five. I was amazed at all these leaders above me in their late fifties and early sixties who were doing nothing but protecting a system they had pioneered twenty years before that was clearly in decline and no longer adding value. The drive to protect their legacy was much stronger than their drive to improve the company's competitive position," said one leader we interviewed. "I never wanted the younger people looking at me saying the things we would say about that generation of leadership."

Leaders are responsible for the goals and visions they set, including how they are achieved. They need to have a perspective that allows for the greatest possible understanding of the context, the situation, the events, and the people.

The greater the scope of their undertaking as a leader, the greater their perspective needs to be. In other words, a leader must be the ultimate generalist (as opposed to specialist). Whatever the industry and organization that leaders are a part of, whatever organizational ladder they are climbing, leaders also need to enrich their understanding of the larger world.

LEADERSHIP COMPETENCIES

In our research into purposeful leadership, we asked our experts in leadership and our highly effective leaders this question: What skills do you use the most that make the biggest difference? We heard the following answers:

Setting the Vision, Goal, or Direction (the Leader's Art)
Goal Oriented
Strategy and Strategic Thinking
Financial Acumen
Resourcing the Strategy with Key People, Investment, and Time

---

Systems Thinking
Setting Policies, Rules, and Managing Culture
Process Orientation
Highly Self-Aware
Highly Self-Regulating
Curious
Open
Selfless
Courageous
Clear Communicator
Socially Adept
Adept Working with Group/Team Dynamics
Judgment and Decision Making
Collaborating with Stakeholders (Cocreating)

LEADERSHIP IDENTITY PROBE

- Do you understand what you are passionate about with respect to your industry?

- How have you been cultivating your leadership growth?

- What do you do to understand and track what is happening in your industry from a technical point of view?

- What do you do to refine and tune your judgment and decision-making capabilities?

- How do you learn about how your customers are changing?

- Where has being an ethical leader required the most courage for you? Has your courage ever failed you? Have you ever sat back and watched an unethical situation happen and not said anything? How good are you at leadership conversations? What's your evidence?

- How good would you be sitting through a full-day conversation critiquing your leadership?

PART FIVE

ACHIEVE

8

GO WHERE YOU
SAID YOU WILL:
STRUCTURE SUCCESS

I am easily satisfied by the very best.

—*Sir Winston Churchill, Prime Minister*
of the United Kingdom (1940–1945)

COMMITMENT: ACHIEVE

Accomplish successful outcomes and deliver excellence
by creating appropriate structure and clarity.

LEARNING SPACES

In the summer of 1969, amid all sorts of turmoil and strife, I watched along with the rest of the world as an American astronaut walked on the moon. The event was the result of President Kennedy standing before Congress in 1961 and proposing the audacious and inspirational goal of landing a man on the moon and returning him safely to the earth before the decade was out. The goal itself has been the fodder of many leadership studies, workshops, articles, and books. What most of us remember is one of the most dramatic, innovative, and revolutionary events of our lives set in the context of troubled, divided, and dark times for the United States as a whole. It was the best and worst of times.

Although the story has been mythologized and elaborated on, it has many elements and many learning points. Yes, a young and inspirational leader created an audacious and fascinating goal. Yes, there were failures and triumphs as well as heroes along the way. And yes, most people don't know the story underneath the story: how the U.S. government structured this exceptional success.

What surprises most people is how much out of the blue this goal came. To say it was disruptive is an understatement. Most of Kennedy's cabinet and advisors were taken completely by surprise and even more dismayed it would totally derail everything else the administration stood for and wanted to achieve: the war on poverty, civil rights, the Cold War. Somehow the goal and the $100 billion estimated cost needed to be integrated into the work of the administration. The members of Kennedy's leadership team had a lot to wrap their minds around and not much time to do it. Where do we get the money? What are the governance procedures required to budget and allocate the money? How do we restructure the cabinet and the leadership? Is this NASA or the military? Is NASA capable of this? Do we have the talent to do this? How and where do we execute this? How do we keep it from becoming political and the members of Congress each wanting the program in their own state?

Although NASA was working on manned space flight with Project Mercury, NASA was not exactly the high-performing organization that we think of today. It was a flawed institution with many public failures. Trust in NASA leadership was not high. Wrapped up in letting NASA implement this goal was a deep need to control the program and its leadership.

As the members of Kennedy's team started to make decisions on how to structure the implementation of the goal, they fought among themselves. The alignment among them was frail at best. But they moved forward with NASA: a year-by-year budget allocation allowing a way forward with other goals, a series of special offices of government to oversee coordination on a global basis, and a realigned White House designed to manage the politics of the space shot—led by then Vice President Johnson. Fortunately for the entire initiative, John Glenn's space flight orbiting earth in 1962 was a rousing success, restoring confidence in NASA and giving Americans a real sense of achievement. The efforts continued, and momentum built throughout the entire Mercury program, as NASA simultaneously announced the acceleration of the Gemini and Apollo programs. The path to the moon had a strategy and a plan. The United States had a coherent plan to achieve the goal. Each successive mission tested new technologies, new techniques, and the limits of human endurance in space.

After Kennedy's assassination, the Johnson leadership team grabbed onto the goal with renewed motivation and inspiration. Fortunately, Johnson was at the helm. He was a master of U.S. bureaucracy and its politics. He infused new money and new talent into NASA, creating a stronger, more effective organization and support system around it. There was not a single member of the Kennedy or Johnson leadership team capable of engineering the United States into space. But what the leadership team could do was structure success.

What Kennedy and Johnson and their respective teams did was set the goal and restructure the current state so the goal could be achieved. They implicitly understood money alone was not going to get the United States to the moon before the Soviet Union. Instead, they reacted to the goal by generating new government structures, infused the whole initiative with talent (including immigrants), created cross-governmental communication and cooperation, created an international network of support from other countries, and built momentum by aggressively focusing NASA on landing a man on the moon—by defunding the majority of its other initiatives.

Kennedy or Johnson could easily have tried to micromanage the whole enterprise. The men could have involved themselves in details in which they had no expertise. Each failure or setback could have sent them into a tailspin, resulting in bad decisions and even more disappointment and delay. They could have seen the whole thing as a direct impact on their egos and their legacies. It's hard to remember just how uncertain, how mysterious, and how scary this whole enterprise was. Instead, and maybe unconsciously, they committed fully to taking everything else they could off NASA's plate to let NASA focus its activity on the goal. And they made sure NASA had everything it needed to succeed. The understanding and discipline of what it means to lead was profound and ultimately delivered superior results. To this day, this focus on structure and organization by leadership remains largely invisible to all but a few scholars of leadership and governance.

GETTING ACHIEVING RIGHT

The highly effective leaders we studied as part of purposeful leadership not only understood the need to multiply achievements and accelerate momentum but also understood it is done by multiplying the number of leaders involved in accomplishing the goal. The larger the enterprise, the larger the number of leaders needing to be engaged and committed to the goal. Leaders who know what they are doing build collectives of leaders. They get comfortable over time, trusting others to achieve the right kinds of things leading to enterprise success.

We call it "delegation," but it really is much more than what we think of when we hear the word "delegation." The highly effective leaders we studied had a balanced approach to all five commitments. This is why they pursued achievement in combination with the other commitments. After determining a great goal, engaging the right talent, and defining the competitive innovation, effective leaders established a structure, delegated power and responsibility, and focused action.

We don't talk about it much in this book, but it is important to understand the biggest and most common mistake made by leaders when it comes to achieving goals: They fail to change the current state. When leaders set an aspirational goal, it is tantamount to success they need to change up what is happening in the present. If the present state were organized correctly, you would already be building momentum toward that big, hairy, audacious goal. Setting the goal should automatically create in a leader's mind the question of how to organize and structure how the goal will be achieved; in other words, how do you change the current state?

Delegate Power and Responsibility

Leadership delegation is the delegation of results, not tasks. It involves keeping each and every function and business working on creating an aligned result with other functions and businesses. It's not so much about "is something getting done" as it is about "is the something getting done being coordinated with all the other things that are getting done," according to the leaders we interviewed. As one leader put it, "You have to totally trust the leaders around you to get things done; it's why you hired them. Keeping it coordinated and integrated is tougher. It's where all your energy should go."

Establish Structure

Just as it's important to trust and to empower others around a goal, you have to establish boundaries to keep things working and progressing. The leaders we talked to started with the "who." Key or critical talent can be spread across too many different projects, initiatives, and businesses. Not all talented people work well together on every type of initiative. Unfortunately, not all leaders are self-aware enough to know which people they do and do not work well with. They often know the people they like to work with. Highly effective leaders know who needs to work with whom on the different types of challenges an organization faces. Some people are "oil and water" on some types of projects, but they are a perfect pairing on other projects.

Structure also includes how often you are going to have a business review or an accountability session on the initiative. Having regular business reviews or project reviews is part of structuring an initiative correctly.

Finally, putting structure to money, process, technology, data usage, and the like is also critical for creating the environment in which people can achieve their goals. Establishing structure is (1) the goal, (2) the people, (3) the reporting, (4) the capital, and (5) the processes and systems.

Focus Action

"When it comes to achieving results, only two things are important: (1) keeping the everyday business delivering effectively, and (2) making the necessary changes happen to make sure you can deliver effectively in the future," reflected one leader in our study. "If you can do these two things, you are getting results." Based on our research, this is not so easy. A great many leaders of the thousands of leaders we have studied struggle with getting things accomplished, and a number of other studies validate our findings. However, our interview data in particular, backed up by our 360-degree data, tells an interesting story.

Leaders who were considered effective were rated highly in inspire, engage, and become. Leaders who were considered ineffective were rated highly in achieve and relatively low in inspire, engage, and become. Leaders who inspire as a focus commitment have less trouble achieving results. It's probably not all that counterintuitive, but behaviorally many leaders continue to focus on achieving in the absence of inspiring.

Interestingly, a young *James* is probably a terrific example of over-focusing on achievement in the absence of inspiration. He often is described as something of a micromanager and too controlling. His focus on the numbers and accountability gives his style a detail orientation and a relentless droning drumbeat. Exit interviews often refer to this style as one of the reasons people leave his organization. On the other side of the ledger, he retains really great people. He is also, of course, masterful at putting the right people on projects, making sure that each project is funded correctly, eliminating distractions, and getting the goals for each initiative exactly right. His overall record of results and process makes him a high-potential leader in his organization.

Priya is the most balanced of our three high potentials. Priya is exceptionally inspiring in communicating what is happening on projects. She engages great talent to work with her, creates a strong culture of innovation, and is excellent in managing her organization's scoreboard and accountabilities. She has a weekly schedule of reviewing every aspect of her projects. In her words, Priya is constantly shaping everyone's contributions.

Jane is more enigmatic on this front: She achieves without micromanaging or providing too much leadership structure or focus. She creates focus in how she structures work arrangements and incentives. She and her organization swarm problems when they arise, and they are their own worst enemy when it comes to creating distractions.

THE LEADER'S ROLE

It's fairly well understood the leader's role is closely associated with creating or setting the vision and the goals of the organization. But the leader's role is also about structuring the success for attaining the goal. Visions and goals must be turned into plans, talent, support, decision structures, timetables, communication mechanisms, and capital. Ultimately, it will boil down to the vision; the strategic design; the managerial design around controls, workflows, and policies; and the operational design around the organizational structure.

It is essential as a leader you know and act upon what needs to change about the current state to create and accelerate momentum toward the goal or vision. If you don't change the current state, you don't reach the goal.

PURPOSE INSIDER

Connie Rath, Clifton Foundation

We all know what it feels like to achieve something. But what can transpire when the components of excellence fuse with the impressionable minds of youth? We caught up with Connie Rath of Clifton Foundation, an organization that uses research and education to further the mission of teaching leaders and researchers to identify and develop strengths in young people. Each partner project has a 10-year goal for growth and impact. Its lab approach is personal, longitudinal, and experience based. Researchers of top strengths accumulate data and stories from schools across the country and then report findings and take action on what works. Rath says:

> When I think about purposeful leadership, there are two parts: the why and the how. The why is a long-term mission and contribution. Any leader of a company should have this in mind. Another thing that purpose means is how you make decisions on a daily basis, asking the "why" question. What is the reason for doing this or that? Purpose becomes daily sorting. It is that long-term mission. At the Clifton Foundation, we're investing in creating better futures for young people. You see a lot of wasted talent in schools and universities. When you can early on figure out strengths in young people, you can help them figure out what they can become. We do a lot of devel-

opmental work with leaders of young people and college students. The students can study their strengths and get options about their future. That is foundational work. I spent twenty-five years as chief human resources officer at Gallup. A lot of success was in the recruiting effort and assuring that people got jobs that fit them well.

I've seen too many poor leaders—and they're probably nonpurposeful—ruin other people, or at least sidetrack them for awhile. The danger is in the effect on the well-being of other people. We're becoming more aware of how the nicks and bruises in the workplace as a result of a poor leader take a toll on a person and that person's family. Then, of course, there is the danger to the organization of that leader making poor decisions.

I'm excited about projects that identify entrepreneurs in high school and bring them together to start a business. I'm in Washington, DC. People here are worried about the city's youth and economic vibrancy. We want to find young people who get excited about starting and growing something, and they get experience as managers and practice what they're doing. Young people need to feel that their talent is valuable. The students who come into our program are loaded with ideas and energy. They don't necessarily have academic talent. Taking advantage of all kinds of talent—especially those talents that are directed toward starting a business or being entrepreneurial inside a business—is one way to teach leadership for the future.

Shivang Vaidya: Chemistry and Ethics

Originally from Navi Mumbai, India, Shivang Vaidya took an "Investing in Strengths" course during his freshman year, motivating him to develop a mentor relationship with Mark Pogue, the former executive director of Nebraska's Clifton Strengths Institute. Then becoming a Strengths Coach changed his approach to self-development and teamwork. During his final semester, he completed 100 one-on-one coaching sessions with students—and learned a great deal about purpose.

First, define a purpose for yourself. Then, understand the individual needs of your team. Where does your purpose and their purpose align? That is key to creating a bond, which assures that you can stick together through challenges or setbacks. My company does employee engagement for small businesses in Nebraska. One of the things I have learned about engagement is understanding what value everyone brings. We also use Gallup's Q12 survey [12 questions that measure the most important elements of employee engagement]. These questions tie directly to performance outcomes. What brings two people together? What is the chemistry level of the team? I decided to go deeper in personal engagement. Someone's beliefs and values are important because they drive decisions. I am also focused on doing the right thing. I want to work with people from a purposeful place. Knowing how that feels, I also think these five commitments should be instilled in high school students.

I believe in mentors, and two purposeful leaders who have mentored me are Gallup's Connie Rath and Jim Clifton [of the Clifton Foundation]. Jim has the goal of helping at least 100 schools and numerous entrepreneurs gain the strengths required to succeed.

Of note, Jim Clifton's father, Don, founded the first-ever "strengths institute" in a business school. The Don Clifton Strengths Institute is located at Don Clifton's alma mater, the University of Nebraska, where he spent 25 years studying, researching, and teaching human development. Clifton concluded that people's weaknesses rarely develop into strengths, but when people develop their inherent strengths, they develop infinitely, leading to productive lives of high value and high well-being. Clifton's legacy is the world-famous Clifton Strengths Finder, which has helped more than 10 million people worldwide learn and develop their strengths. The assessment has been used by most Fortune 1000 companies, NGOs such as the World Bank and United Nations, and many federal government agencies and departments, including the military.

Vaidya adds: "You have to do something to become someone. Wanting is not good enough. We need to change the way we think in order to achieve. You can't depend on everything that is external. You must do everything in your power to become someone."

Jasie Beam: Community
Is Her Number Six Commitment

What comes to mind as I look at these five commitments of purposeful leadership is that I see each of these commitments embodied by all the leaders that I look up to. Without any of these commitments, a good leader lacks the ability to effectively lead a team or a project. These five commitments are universal. When I think about group projects in my time as a student, the best group projects had a leader who embodied all of these commitments. The same can be said for a company manager, a teacher, a parent, or a community leader. So, these commitments are widely applicable.

I was inspired by my love for my town, Gering, Nebraska, a town of about 8,000 people that is basically supported by our neighboring town of Scottsbluff. Gering doesn't have many stores or other economy-boosting opportunities, so all our money is spent in Scottsbluff because that is where everything is. It is hard to improve Gering's economy, schools, downtown district, etc., when all the money is being funneled into a different town. So, because I love Gering so much, I wanted to think of ways to help Gering grow, instead of just providing Scottsbluff with the means to grow. That's where the whole idea came from—not just wanting to live in Gering, but to truly support Gering by providing economic opportunities that it lacks. There are a few small shops and one grocery store in Gering, but there is not enough to keep Gering residents from just heading to Scottsbluff when they need something. It would take a large project and many more businesses than just one to make Gering the final destination, but slowly it could help provide Gering residents the opportunity to stay in town instead of heading to Scottsbluff.

My original idea for this revitalization was to open a coffee shop in Gering. There are two coffee shops currently in Gering, but neither place really provides a place of community; they're more just a grab-and-go experience. So, I wanted to have a large space for teenagers to come after school or for business professionals to have meetings or lunches. Teenagers don't have anything to do after school in Gering and could greatly benefit from having a safe place to spend their afternoons. I wanted programming for the students so they would be able to benefit from the coffee shop beyond just sitting around drinking coffee. This would provide not only economic benefit for the services that I could funnel back into the community but would also provide benefit for each student's development, which would have long-term benefits on the community since the students are the future residents and decision makers of Gering.

Another major piece of my coffee shop would be an event space. Currently, there are only two event spaces in Gering. So, birthday parties, graduation ceremonies, wedding receptions, and other celebrations have limited options. The current event spaces are designed more like a stiff meeting space with room dividers, which have no personality. My event space would provide opportunities for smaller gatherings like birthday parties, and for personalization and character to be infused into the actual space. I have played around with a lot of ideas for the coffee shop: activities for community members; meeting rooms for professionals to rent; event space to hold weddings, birthday parties, etc.; and much more. I have not completely vetted these ideas through market research, but I have evaluated the market and found possible locations for the building and other logistical information.

The traits that are important for me in leaders are trust, respect, compassion, drive, and vision. All these things are also embodied in the five commitments of a purposeful leader. If I meet a leader whom I do not trust, I will not be dedicated to helping their vision because there would be a lack of a foundational relationship. The same can be said for respect; if it is lacking, there is no foundation for a relationship. If you know that your leader does not care or lacks compassion, then it is nearly impossible to be a dedicated follower. If a leader doesn't have the drive or will to take on a task themselves, it is hard for me to be motivated to do that for them. Finally, a leader without a vision is hard to follow because you wouldn't know where they are leading you. All of these factors are encompassed in the five commitments of a purposeful leader and are invaluable for any successful leader to have.

It's hard to choose just a few leaders that I look up to because leaders can present themselves in many different situations. I'd say that the most prominent leaders in my life are my parents, my grandparents, and my mentors at the University of Nebraska–Lincoln. My parents and grandparents all have built such trust and respect throughout my life with me that it would be impossible not to look up to them. They have been there for absolutely every part of my life, the highs and lows and everywhere in between. They all embody the five commitments to the exact definition. They inspire me to work toward my goals. They allow me to always work through my passions to help me thrive in everything that I do; they have given me the freedom to imagine my own future and support that vision. They also celebrate my achievements no matter how small they may seem, and they give me the strength and courage to always grow in my abilities. My mentors at the University of Nebraska–Lincoln have helped me grow professionally and personally. There is a saying, "You grow up more in one year of college than you do in all four years of high school." The mentors that I have met during my time at school have seen me through all that development and helped me foster the development in the most productive and individual way. They, like my family, also encompass each of the five commitments, which allows me to follow their leadership confidently.

Transformation takes time, but it can be accelerated. Leaders essentially become their own change agents, reflecting on their commitments and adapting. The more you are surrounded by other purposeful leaders, the more your future will unfold and amplify.

PURPOSE INSIDER

Committed to Achieve

Purposeful leadership can be embedded in a brand. When you think of motorcycles, what brand comes to mind as the industry leader? But what does Harley-Davidson have to do with purposeful leadership? An explicit definition, says Julie Anding, an executive at Harley-Davidson, and we're glad to learn of it:

These leadership models live in a cultural context, and the words may mean something different in different cultural contexts. How do you manage for that? People will associate their own meaning to the words. At Harley-Davidson, it is all about legacy, 150 years of history. And we are committed to passing on a healthy company to the future. Our leader takes it personally, so I want to be part of the legacy. He is working on setting the stage for the next five to ten years of where we are heading. The leader I am thinking of is really good at putting ideas into a story.

Also good at pulling a few people together, he seeks input from key people that will help to make whatever initiative we are working on better. He is passionate when he tells the story. He is animated, positive, engaging, and he inspires you to get on board with him and make Harley-Davidson better. He is self-less and passionate.

Engage is interesting, particularly with the Millennials. There is a sense that Millennials want to be pulled in and engaged. Having a leader do that is important. The idea of engage and involve different generations to achieve takes skill and finesse, and this is not the same for all talents.

Harley-Davidson is one of those companies that we constantly hear about: successful and always in some sort of transformation, changing with the times and the culture. This constant renewal is evidence pointing to the quality and effectiveness of its leaders—setting big goals and visions, engaging people, innovating, and finding new ways to structure things to create success. The company may be more than 150 years old, but it remains fresh and modern. Leadership has a unique capability to honor the past, keep an eye on the future, and focus on the present.

ACHIEVE PROBE

- Who are your "usual suspects" when it comes to getting things done? Whom are you overlooking?

- How does your ego or need for control get in the way of your "team" functioning effectively?

- Do you ever believe that you are more capable than your staff, that only you know how to get things done, that things always have to be done a certain way (your way)?

- Do you ever underestimate or oversimplify the time, the investment, the resources, or the difficulty it will take your team to get something done? Why do you think you do this?

- How do you mentor your leaders to be effective in organizing people around goals?

- How do you go about evaluating what's working and what's not in your organization?

- Are you more likely to "play it safe" and take on work that you know you can achieve, or do you look for work that is challenging, exciting, growth oriented, and risky?

- Are you known as a great collaborator?

9

POWER OR PURPOSE (ALWAYS KNOW THE DIFFERENCE!)

Those who have great power should use it lightly.

—*Seneca the Younger, philosopher and dramatist*

EXHILARATION OR EXHAUSTION

The most implicit and dominant dogma of leadership is rooted in the ideas of leadership as hierarchy, power, influence, and authority. This dogma presupposes that the leader is competent, even expert, in how things should be done. It also assumes that the leader is the smartest individual in the organization that they lead. In most models, the leader's power comes from the role and level of his or her job in the organization and power comes from the individual at the top of the pyramid. No wonder this characterization can also inspire fear.

Some, not all, of us buy into this dogma when we enter leadership roles. We are so hungry to accomplish things in our new leadership role that we inadvertently fall into this set of assumptions to make it happen. When we are frustrated by the slowness or the difficulty of leading, we may take shortcuts. For those who don't believe this dogma, a cocktail of visionary, goal-directed, principled leadership combined with hierarchical leadership secures results.

Power is the capacity to take action. Power means that you have the necessary and requisite authority or decision-making rights to bring together people, information, money, and other materials and make the decision to fund something, invest in something, hire someone, fire someone, say yes and no, say go or no-go. In many ways, "power" is not a clear term: The concept is confusing, vague, and somewhat complex and connotes different ideas to different people. My mentor used to define power as "the ability to poke the future in a different direction." He really changed my negative perception of power into something with a comforting charm to it.

I've learned over many years is power is neither positive nor negative, neither good nor bad. It's how power is used that makes it good or bad, not the power itself. When power is used ethically and fairly, it can be seen as a good thing. Of course, when leaders have the power to make something better and they withhold power for whatever reason, then a different picture of power comes into play.

There is no question leaders in any organization must understand power is an important tool in their toolbox. Leaders must recognize their power, must know how to use it effectively and ethically, and must understand how to augment its positive impacts and diminish its negative impacts. Although power is an abstract concept, leaders can make it quite real and tangible in a decision. Maybe even more abstract is the idea of distributing power. Power can be distributed across levels, geographies, businesses, functions, and people. Power can come from many sources: position power, expertise power, relationship power, informational power, referent power, coercive power, and reward power.

The exercise of power presents a leader with a three-way dilemma: Do I use my power and authority? Or do I use my personal influence? Or do I create a vision and engage people? While this may seem a false dilemma because most leaders will use all their tools, the dilemma presents different challenges, consequences, and potentially different outcomes. These differences are all the result of how stakeholders react and close the feedback loop on the leader. If you examine the social contract implied in each of the three dilemmas, you derive the following:

• Power and authority may beget compliance.

• Influence may beget cooperation.

• Visionary, purposeful leadership may beget engagement.

Leaders need to make choices on how to get things done based on the culture of the company, the individuals in question, and the challenge in front of them. Our research shows leadership is a reciprocal relationship. Leaders impact stakeholders. Stakeholders engage and impact leaders. The feedback loop continues to hum and create cycles of leadership goodness. Purposeful, principled leadership based on a vision is powerful. Purposeful leadership really means you're a leader sometimes and a follower sometimes: The power to get things done is in the relationship and the feedback loop. When you are able to create a collective of leaders guided by a shared vision and set of goals, you are creating a force capable of poking the future in a different direction.

James is learning how to manage power. At this stage of his career, he is a bit of a split personality. With his reliable network of loyal leaders that report to him on his team, he takes a purposeful approach and shares power carefully. With the remaining leaders on his team, he is a highly authoritative leader. With his peers, he is careful to take the time and have the conversations with them; in other words, he tries to be influential. It is time consuming and frustrating, and it doesn't always work. It is a pattern or a style he is only just becoming aware of and trying to change. He fights his instincts every day to try to be different with his peers and others. He is continually frustrated and disengaged when he feels his efforts are not getting results with other people. His frustration kicks him into "expert mathematician" mode, often making the relationship and the outcome worse, not better. To his credit, he sees how his power style impacts the world, and he is working on it.

Priya is all vision and energy She speaks in analogies, metaphors, and stories. Her warmth and her energy come through with an ensemble of incredibly talented engineers and architects. She chooses inspiring clients who want to build inspiring buildings, and she encourages her team to create more value by "making great even better." She rarely has to pull out her authority card when working with her team on client projects. Organizationally, of course, she does pull out her authority card and her influence card when she perceives the organization hindering her business progress. And we already know she has to deal with backlash.

Jane is a bit of an enigma when it comes to her deployment of her power. She absolutely overplays her expert power. She has been the quintessential decisive leader in dealing with organizational challenges around bias and harassment. She is fair, equitable, and compassionate in her people decisions. However, she is unclear when she delegates authority and can often override decisions others make, even when they have been given the authority. Her vision is vague, and though she is expert and clear on the technical side of running a call center, she is equally unclear and tentative in governing an organization.

Power is such a complex topic. It has been written about endlessly by novelists, screenwriters, playwrights, and academics for centuries, and yet it remains mysterious and unknowable. What's particularly unknowable is how each of us will handle power when we actually have it. How will we handle ourselves? Will we succumb to its obvious temptations? Will we become a cliché? Of all the aspects of leadership, the examination of power is the one that brings to mind how much of leadership mystery is wrapped up in this idea of how each of us manages power. Will we be able to master the moments when temptations spontaneously but systematically challenge us? How will we poke the future?

PURPOSE INSIDER

General Darren W. McDew

General McDew was commander of the U.S. Transportation Command at Scott Air Force Base in Illinois from 2015 to 2018. USTRANSCOM is the single manager for global air, land, and sea transportation for the Department of Defense, so McDew's assignments varied widely. He is known for his leadership philosophy of keen self-awareness, personal development, and a constant eye on innovation. Sharing his insights, he notes:

> Once you put on a uniform, you're a leader. The same is true in the civilian sector. Sometimes we forget that the military is an organization with strong boundaries between who is allowed in and who is excluded. When you cross over into the world of the military, you are in a foreign environment. This means that you have to start at the beginning and hit each step on leadership scales with people, and military leadership is mostly about people and the ability to inspire people. One of the biggest difficulties is ambiguity; you have to make a ton of decisions with inexact data and based on your own experience. With ambiguity, the biggest thing is understanding the risks and who's assuming those risks and then thinking about who the risks affect and what is at stake (lives). You can't be paralyzed by ambiguity. I *will* make a decision based on risk and my experience.
>
> The most important leadership lesson I've learned during my career has been the value of personal and professional growth: diverse assignments, learning, reading; knowing who I am and who I am not. Over my career, I have become more aware. I listen. I pay attention to people not speaking. I know more about the types of things that press someone's buttons. When you don't acknowledge who you are, you tend to shy away from things you are not good at. Example: I'm an operational leader, a civil engineer. People in

this space like facts and analytics. It's less personal. So I force myself to get personal. I begin and end a conversation with a thank you to people. Analytically, I wouldn't naturally do it, but I know I need to.

I think the work [Linkage] has done is amazing, particularly the five commitments and journey. For me, achievement fits right into my wheelhouse. It's where I'm most comfortable. But you can't get anywhere unless you inspire and engage. Innovation and achievement then flow from that.

I inspire and focus on people. I spent a year at Sun Microsystems, two years at the White House, two at the Senate, and the knowledge of how to inspire and the fact that you have to inspire is not as present in the civilian sector. The level of structure in the military makes it both easier and tougher to inspire and engage, as we have set command. The top 10% performers in both the military and civilian sectors believe discipline is a stronger influence in the military than in corporate settings, and that level of discipline is a big difference. We do acknowledge everyone as a leader, and discipline is hard wired from day one.

What factors do I believe to be most important when considering an officer for promotion? Universally: Potential, I tend to look at past performance as a barometer for future potential. Next, I consider assignments and how you do as well as schools we sent you to. Along the way, you can see who does the assignments better than their peers and accelerate the ones who are outperforming.

> My advancement was purely performance based. I never applied for a job in my life. I was sitting at my desk in the Pentagon and saw that there was going to be an opening in the White House. The hiring manager knew five or six guys who would be perfect and told them to apply. I was nominated by a former boss. Working in the White House, I learned how to get things done through influence, without positional power. Treat everybody well, and it works out.

Purposeful Leaders let the vision, the goals, and the plan be the power. They inspire, they engage and let others contribute their ideas and their talents, they encourage people and support them in breaking the status quo in order to get the momentum going, and they put the right people together in the right combinations to make it happen.

POWER PROBE

- In your current role, define your power. What decisions can you make without getting permission (this is not the same as informing) from a superior?

- In looking back at your leadership history, what have been your most positive "power" practices?

- What has been your most negative experience in using your power?

- If you were to interview five to seven former direct reports, what three words would they use to describe how you wield power as a leader?

- Why do you think you might revert to power as opposed to such positive, purposeful leadership practices as inspiration, empowerment, and inclusion?

PART SIX

BECOME

10

LEADING WITH PURPOSE: PUTTING IT ALL TOGETHER

All of the great leaders evidence four basic qualities that are central to their ability to lead: adaptive capacity, the ability to engage others through shared meaning, a distinctive voice, and unshakeable integrity. These four qualities mark all exemplary leaders, whatever their age, gender, ethnicity, or race.

—Warren G. Bennis

> ## COMMITMENT: BECOME
> *Grow with determination, compassion,*
> *self-awareness, and courage.*

Throughout this book, we've tried to articulate and explore the commitments that leaders need to make and keep to succeed with their vision and goals. But leadership is not a one-way street. Leaders don't dictate, demand, and direct—not effective ones anyway. The leaders of today build a two-way street with their stakeholders, a feedback loop with stakeholders of expectations, contributions, and commitments. With proper care and conversation, these feedback loops create a huge accumulation of goodness: customer loyalty, product quality, profitability, employee engagement, community engagement, industry respect, and economic contributions to a town, a city, a state, or a region. One of the first leaders I was able to observe firsthand, William J. O'Brien, used to say to me that "leaders, above all, have the capacity to take what they learn and apply it. They, above all, create the reinforcing loop where leaders challenge followers to up their game, and followers then challenge leaders to up their game. And what happens creates the right result." But Bill also would say that leaders need to want to create the right results. "Human capital drives financial capital," he would posit, "and not the other way around."

As I think back on all the things Bill was able to teach me and the much smaller number of things that I actually learned, what he taught me is leadership is, first and foremost, about the right goals; second, it is about feedback loops that reinforce or create virtuous cycles; third, it is about accumulations of goodness; and fourth, it is about humanity. Underlying all this, he taught me leadership is, above all, a shift of mind: a change in what you value, what you think, and what you then do. He would say, "A shift of mind, a shift of character, and a lifelong 'journey.'" And while there is a journey around learning to inspire others, engage others, innovate, and achieve, there is a deeper journey in learning to "become."

So whether you are a leader of a small community, a not-for-profit company, a larger for-profit company, or just someone trying to create change in an institution of some kind, we found four human-centric practices that are central to becoming a purposeful leader:

- **SELF-AWARENESS.** The capability to understand and leverage yourself in working with people, teams, and organizations.

- **RESPECT.** The capability to bring out the best in others by focusing on their talents, feelings, and interests. Above all, it is a deep respect for every individual.

- **COURAGE.** The willingness to show yourself and your values regardless of risk, to speak truth, and to be bold in your vision As has been said by hundreds of leadership experts before me, courage is the willingness to act despite your fears and in the face of humiliation, or the potential of being ostracized, or financial risk to oneself or one's family. Joseph Campbell wrote, "The cave you fear to enter holds the treasure you seek."

- **COMMITMENT.** The sense of high personal responsibility, hard work, determination, and personal discipline while working for success. Commitment is about being the "role model." Ultimately though, commitment is about the focus and adaptability required to achieve a big goal.

It isn't that we philosophically decided leaders need to be respectful, courageous, self-aware, and committed. This isn't some armchair decision we made about leaders and leadership. After inspiration, the leaders who were rated the most effective in our study scored highest in these four practices of "become." When we sorted through our interview data with leaders, leadership experts, and leadership development experts, major themes that leapt off the page were leaders were the individuals who consistently took the more difficult personal path rather than the easy path. Leaders were the self-disciplined ones. Leaders were the compassionate ones. Leaders were respectful. Leaders were the ones who were inclusive. Leaders treated *everyone* as special, regardless of their position. Leaders paid attention to people. They were the confident ones. Leaders were the people who engaged with others and took them and their questions seriously.

Leaders, they almost universally agreed, were the ones who made almost any situation better. Whether it was walking into a meeting that had gone sour, a conflict between two or three peers, a team drifting into dysfunction, or a business needing a turn-around—leaders made it work better. Leaders have the capacity to take what they have learned and what they know and apply it to the challenge in front of them in a positive, inspiring way. In addition, we cannot forget one of the expectations followers have of leaders is simple: We want our leaders to be good people. I want to say despite all the difficulties and challenges that leaders have to deal with every day, in a certain indefinable but unique way, they bring joy to what they and their stakeholders do.

Patti Smith, the songwriter and artist known as the punk rock poet, once wrote that "if you feel good about who you are, it will radiate." Leaders have much to contend with regardless of the size of their enterprise. Challenges will constantly change, evolve, get more complex, and grow more demanding. I love the expression that I once heard that leaders have to deal with a lot of C-R-A-P: criticism, resistance, a-------, and pressure. There is no better message that I can convey about leadership and being a leader than it is important for you as a leader to feel good about yourself, who you are, what drives and motivates you, how you interact with the world, and what you are trying to accomplish—your sense of purpose.

Leaders must have the identity and presence to be credible in who they are and their vision. It must come from inside you, and if it does, it will "radiate." In essence, "Radiate your inspiration!"

I was explaining purposeful leadership to a group of leaders in an engineering company a few months ago. After I finished and was taking questions, one engineer said to me (I had to write it down it was so perfect), "Am I understanding you correctly that if we over-optimize on the axis of achievement, that we will negatively impact what we are trying to do, but if we overoptimize on becoming an inspiring leader, we will at least have a higher probability of success?" The room cracked up with laughter.

"Yes," I said, "if your identity and purpose are something that you feel really good about, you will infect others, build their inner resourcefulness, and create a virtuous cycle of accumulating achievements. What a leader does is offer stakeholders a relationship to build a narrative and a call to action around the future. What a leader does is say to people that it's hard but that we can make it better together."

LEARNING LEADERSHIP

James has been slow, and to be honest, cynical, to accept this idea around becoming an inspiring leader. He seemed most motivated by financial results and would sometimes come across as a mercenary. He was perceived as not really being emotionally connected to what his organization did. He was perceived as pure ambition, yet simultaneously seen as a high-potential leader. Also, while his

organization suffered a higher than average turnover for his company, James still managed to build and sustain a core group of people who believed in him and what he was trying to do in marketing.
People, particularly the executives in his organization, agreed with
his point of view around marketing, saw his capabilities in building a solid team of people who could contribute, appreciated the
innovations they had created together, and were pleased with the
trends in the results. And despite the outer shell, what they also
saw was someone with good judgment, someone who really didn't
come across as having a big ego, someone who would courageously
stand up for doing the right thing for his people and who handled
quite a number of difficult people issues with resiliency, and someone who had built a marketing organization that made the company better. While there was the hard exterior he showed, many
people in the organization could tell tales of his kindness and his
generosity. He was introverted and often misread because of this,
and yet he was a confident, committed leader in the organization.
For the moment, his organization wants to see him fully develop
the potential of marketing.

Priya represents someone who had truly become a force for
her beliefs around how the construction industry should do things.
She clearly understood the reasons why people and companies
didn't like contractors. She understood that she was in an industry that mostly underperformed relative to customer expectations,
which weren't high to begin with.

She understood the call to action. She had spent years building the engineering and business expertise to be successful. She
understood herself pretty well. She had built a network of relationships across the industry and could easily bring the right people
together for a project. She was great at coordinating people and
entities to make things work in terms of their contributions. She

was the epitome of someone who knew the rules and could recombine and rework the rules in innovative ways to do projects that others felt were either impossible or impossible for the budget. She also understood that she was a woman in what was historically a man's world, a minority. In many ways, Priya found more acceptance outside her organization than inside it. Compared with the average male contractor, she was extraordinarily business savvy and customer savvy. She was an exceptionally qualified engineer, but the people she hired were empowered to make highly valuable contributions to projects. She swooned over details but could helicopter up to the big picture as deftly as anyone else. Mostly, what always came through with Priya was her love for people. She loved meeting clients, going to industry events, speaking at her different alumni clubs, working at career events for her company, mentoring young talent in the organization. There was true joy in these types of things for her.

Nevertheless, Priya was equally irritated and frustrated when her company asked her to do "dumb" things or when certain functions established policies and rules for the whole organization that only served themselves. While a certain population loved her "courage" in fighting the dumb bureaucracy, there were others who believed she was a short-term thinker who could not see the long-term value in their policies and rules, and they were not supportive of her.

The executives, particularly her CEO, fortunately saw Priya differently. Her organization has been unusually successful in attracting female engineers. The women in the organization see her as their courageous champion. This was not overlooked by her CEO. The CEOs of the companies that Priya's organization built buildings for universally respected her and requested her as their project lead. She had a great reputation in the industry associations to which she belonged. City officials where she had done business were remarkably complimentary of her.

Could Priya be a little more self-aware of some of the things she does that create a lot of noise in the organization? Could she mature a bit in how she handles certain organizational issues? Could a promotion accelerate some of her development needs? Could her CEO spend more time with her and shape some of these behaviors? Clearly, he was betting it could all happen for her.

Jane is also a high potential with a good growth trajectory. She is a warm, humble, and social person. Her expertise in call center management is unrivaled. But everyone who knows her well knows she is also a bit of a "hot mess." She brings tremendous brainpower and expertise to everything she does, but she's also disorganized, never knows what time it is, and can be incredibly reactive to certain types of events. She's kind of an enigma because she can also get in a meeting and look at a certain problem with a systematic and penetrating intelligence. There are times when she can get so deeply into an issue that she can be perceived as harsh and uncaring, even disrespectful.

When Jane learns she has hurt people or caused everyone in the organization some pain, she tries hard to fix it. Unfortunately, sometimes she doesn't quite hit the mark. And while Jane has definitely learned the cost of heroics and reactivity, she isn't 100 percent there yet. In her organization, Jane is also considered a hero and a champion to other women.

Jane's identity is highly wrapped up in her call center expertise, to the point where executive management wonders if she has what it takes to step up a level and be a true banker and embrace what the larger organization is all about. The executives are engaging her by putting her on some whole organization committees as well as having her serve as a mentor to some younger leaders in different parts of the business. Long term, they see her as a potential successor to the organization's COO, maybe not the current COO, but down the road. She will need to widen her business focus and communication capabilities to make this happen. Just as importantly, she will need to get better at systematically bringing out the best in others in a more positive way. "What we are really focused on with Jane is her overall learning agility. She has so much brainpower, we hope she can turn some of it on herself," says her CEO. "She is still young, so we have a long runway to help her. She's clearly one of our best-performing and highest-potential leaders."

Ethical Decision Making

Perhaps one area where all three leaders are seen as particularly strong is their ethics.

All three of these leaders are known for the fairness of their judgment. While each has various strengths and weaknesses, the narrative around their ethics goes in the right direction. Each is known as a truth teller. They all have a strong ability to see the reality of their worlds and describe the current state of their worlds accurately, objectively, and fairly—pointing out their own mistakes equally in the process.

Although Priya struggles a bit with her ego at times, Jane and James are known to leave their egos at the door when they come to work in the morning. All three have a strong core-principled approach to handling conflicts of interest and working with people when making decisions to ensure that self-interest is not in play, including for themselves. Now, while James struggles with purpose-driven decisions, he is generally a great role model and has built a great leadership culture. There are some strains of an "old boy network" that occasionally are part of James's team, but when he becomes aware of these issues, he generally does a great job of addressing them. Unfortunately, he is still learning to see them before they develop. Of course, he does occasionally slip and lead from his power, dictating what people need to do.

Jane, in contrast, can struggle with her leadership culture. She has created a strong program of customer education for her call center focused around a core of ethics. Jane herself is an outstanding role model for the power of fairness and equity in how she makes her own decisions. She just struggles in scaling this to the whole organization.

There is one area in particular where all three leaders are considered outstanding: All three are known to fight for fairness and equity, not just in their own organization but in the larger organizations in which they are members.

Priya, in particular, has been an outstanding champion of women and other diverse populations. She works across her organization mentoring and sponsoring talented individuals, often bringing them into her organization when she has the opportunity and capability. To the irritation and frustration of her peers, she is a truth teller when she sees unfairness and bias operating in their functions. As a result, Priya has made enemies in HR for calling out lapses in judgment and bias in certain selection and promotion processes. Her CEO applauds her courage and conviction and admits to learning from her how to approach various challenging issues.

James, in his own way, is constantly in search of great talent, rooting out bad leaders quickly. His decisions around people are objective and centered on metrics where he can find them and use them. Although he wouldn't call it a meritocracy, he has indeed created a marketing organization where the talented rise regardless of their diverse characteristics and the average are quickly rooted out, also regardless of their diversity. While he can struggle with diffusion of responsibility, talented individuals are given plenty of responsibility and empowerment. His current organization is 70 percent women, and his direct reports are 65 percent men. He is quick to complain and even struggle with the traditional methods used to develop leaders. Time, role progression, and diversity around responsibilities simply do not produce leaders fast enough for him, leading him to sometimes throw talent into roles and responsibilities that are beyond them. While James believes his "sink-or-swim" methods are successful, HR believes otherwise.

Jane simply struggles with building a leadership culture that is effective. She relies on her heroes in the organization to do the right thing, as they almost always do.

The organization she took over was rife with gender discrimination and had four times the number of harassment suits as the rest of the bank. There were a number of leaders reporting to her that were not helping the situation, remaining mute about the problems being created by their friends or their more productive workers.

When Jane took over, the call center had fewer than a hundred people. Still, as she assessed the organization, she found many instances of abuse of power. The multiple acquisitions that soon followed allowed Jane to find and promote more talented and fair leaders—many of whom were "in her image." As the organization grew past 500 people on three shifts, her problems were less about bad leaders and more about the gaps in her good leaders around organizational systems and processes that were not directly a function of managing customer calls. So while she has absolutely turned the call center around, she still has approximately 70 percent of her leaders who are oriented around managing calls instead of managing people. She had unwittingly created an organization of firefighters and heroes. As she and her executives look forward, they are hoping to shape Jane into more of a leader with an organizational purpose, one who develops great leaders and talent for the bank and not just the call center. In Jane's organization, diffusion of responsibility is more the issue. No one seems to take ownership of creating a high-reliability organization. No one seems to really understand how to create a human capital plan that isn't reactive. As Jane's awareness and understanding have grown around this issue, she has been seeking out learning opportunities for herself, including hiring an executive coach.

Emotional Presence and Self-Awareness

Our three leaders are also better at seeing people. Priya, James, and Jane are all excellent at being able to see people and their motivations. They are insightful at seeing the personal and political agendas, the self-interest, and the self-promoting behaviors that anyone at anytime can unexpectedly bring to the table. They are also surprisingly able to cut through these behaviors and shape them into something that contributes to the team and the organization. They are well versed in pulling introverted, quiet, or cautious people out of their shells. They help to instill confidence in employees and a sense that their contributions are required, even *imperative*. While some people might see the more aggressive people and the more introverted people as separate groups, Priya, Jane, and James all perceive both groups as interconnected. Each, as leader, determines the game and the rules and can actually direct the purpose of the game and shape the behavior positively. In a different way, they understand that a single team member with strong self-interest can do tremendous damage to the overall results of the team, especially if the team member is successful in his or her endeavors.

James and Jane are learning creating strong, centralized control as a means of countering the rogue behavior of high performers may not work. Both struggle with finding the balance in their own actions to create a healthy, optimal organization. Jane is often quoted as saying that the more deeply she sees the complexity of her organization, the more it reveals even greater complexities that she doesn't understand.

Where Priya, James, and Jane have growing to do is in self-awareness. Priya is the most advanced of the three in her understanding of her strengths and weaknesses and how she uses herself as a lever for building better outcomes. James continues trying to find his purpose other than his love of marketing. Jane struggles with how she contributes to the organization's issues through her beliefs, her understanding of her role, and her actions. Her reactiveness is getting better over time, but she still wrestles with how she can change her reactiveness and address key issues. Her coach is working hard to help Jane understand that sometimes the more obvious lever in a system can create counterintuitive effects. Her coach is helping Jane to stop overreacting and overcorrecting when certain issues arise in her organization. To Jane's credit, she is beginning to develop new habits, reducing the number of meetings she holds, supporting her direct reports more, and keeping the messaging positive and big picture.

Global Mindset

While Priya, James, and Jane are building their sense of self-awareness, they are simultaneously learning how these complex organizations can be counterintuitive in how they react to leadership, competition, economic fluctuations, popular cultural events, and the politics that govern the U.S. economy.

We tend to compartmentalize each of these things as separate and independent, but they are all interdependent, and the boundaries we think are there don't really exist. This is a major lesson for any leader. And leaders must understand the limits of their own worldview or perspective as well. In our interviews with leadership experts, we were surprised how often they mentioned how curious and well read their leadership exemplars were, and how global those exemplars were in their thinking, rarely if ever compartmentalizing problems or creating false boundaries. They truly saw the global or holistic nature of the enterprise they led. They were perceptive in understanding where the real boundaries were between the different functions or teams in the organization. Really adept leaders understand grouping people into a team or a function and giving it a name doesn't mean that it exists as an island unto itself; purposeful leaders quickly understand when a problem has crossed between departments and was neither department's fault.

Our expert interviewees were quick to point out that the best leaders they have seen had tremendous mental flexibility and could quickly change their thinking with each new presentation or each new problem brought to the executive team. One leadership development expert we interviewed posited truly great leaders were extremely perceptive in sorting out how the artificiality we create with functional and business boundaries can create problems rather than solve them. These perceptive leaders were constantly in search of new organizational structures and designs. Rather than think about each piece of the organization as a single neat piece unto itself, they understood how the multiple pieces together produced multiple outcomes.

Learning Agility

We cannot stop change.

Everything is constantly changing, and the complexity of all that change is increasing. There is a lot of stuff to make sense of that doesn't necessarily make sense. Russell Ackoff, the legendary operations theorist, wrote: "[Leaders] are not confronted with problems that are independent of each other, but with dynamic situations that consist of complex systems of changing problems that interact with each other. I call such situations messes. . . . [Leaders] do not solve problems, they manage messes."

This entanglement of complexity means that the world a leader perceives is uncertain and ambiguous and increasingly likely to change rapidly. Making sense of this change and complexity requires leaders who can adapt and learn as they continue to strive for their goals. It requires them to be innovative or to stimulate others to innovation as they perceive all these messes, trends, and new technologies. But learning cannot be separated from having a global mindset, emotional presence, and ethical judgment.

Jane, the youngest of our three leaders, struggles the most with complexity. Her path to scaling up her leadership will require her to find a way to eliminate heroics while finding ways for the organization to become more collaborative. James needs to create a more participative leadership style as he grows and develops. Priya needs to manage the system of relationships better as she takes on new challenges in her career.

All of them will need to continue to refine the clarity and inspirational nature of their vision. They are incredibly intelligent leaders, and they will eventually figure out how to scale themselves and their leadership lessons.

To Become or Not to Become

Leaders who are developed and formed in most leadership development systems are likely to think leadership is about power and control and prediction. They think that, as they assume leadership roles and responsibilities, their role is to be the answer, to solve problems.

When I first took a leadership role, or maybe even my first two or three leadership roles, I furiously believed that I was there to solve the problems, control the organization, and manage the budget. I didn't understand that I was there to achieve goals and develop the organization and the talent. I believed I was playing whack-a-mole with all the problems the organization suffered. It was interesting how easy, relatively speaking, it was to identify the problems, and how hard it became to structure and implement good solutions. First, it was surprising how many people who worked for me didn't (or wouldn't) listen to me. Second, it was even more fascinating how many of my great solutions spawned even more problems. It may sound funny, but I just thought I was getting dumber and dumber as time went on. I lost confidence in myself. I stopped trusting others. I introverted terribly.

Now, when all this was apparent but had not done any consequential, irreversible damage, my mentor showed up in my office doorway and said, "Let's have lunch." His ability to show up and ask me to lunch just after I really needed him mystifies me to this day. Of course, he further wormed his way into my heart by asking all sorts of questions and never giving me any good answers. He passed away more than a decade ago, and I never really said thank you to him for the role he played in forming me as a leader. His work—and the contributions of thinkers like Donella Meadows, Peter Senge, Bill O'Brien, and Marvin Weisbord—helped me find my principles of leadership. My mentor helped me learn that leadership is not about mastering prediction and control but about reaching for goals. We as leaders can bring our purpose and our principles to an organization, a business, a function, or a team, and together, through leadership, we can bring forth something better, more positive, and more balanced across all of our stakeholders than could ever be produced by our belief in ourselves as levers of control.

I began this book by talking about how cynical and distrusting we have become about leaders and leadership. I want to end by putting forth a few lessons I have learned about leading and learning to lead. Some of these lessons have a lot of cuts and bruises behind them. Some of these lessons I learned virtually by watching others succeed or fail. Some are thought experiments that I got to play out in real life, and for which I got rewarded for trying them (although I won't tell you how the experiments really turned out).

I believe strongly that leaders are here to achieve goals and create all sorts of goodness for their organizations, their products, their cultures, and their people. I also maintain that leadership is a two-way relationship. One that is maintained by conversation: the informal exchange of ideas.

My leadership lessons, combined with the commitments and practices of purposeful leadership, are still a work in progress. By worldview I am a humanist. And even though I am offering principles, I generally prefer evidence-based thinking.

We are all here to learn and, I hope, challenge. We commit to continue to try to figure out leaders and leadership. I hope this book gives you the opportunity to renew and engage with leadership in a new way. It's the best I can hope for. The great Satchel Paige once said, "Dance like no one is watching." I say, "Lead because they are watching! "In leadership, you are always being observed. Your actions must match your words. It's not what you say; it's what you do.

In this amazing time of change, volatility, and ambiguity, we were surprised to learn in our interviews with leadership development experts and leadership experts that not only do leaders have a "why," but they have a "how." The patterns of how they lead, the transparency with which they lead, and the self-management were telltale signs of powerful habits of purposeful leadership.

The how in most cases boiled down to a simple set of ideas that governed their behavior as a leader. Somewhere in their leadership careers they had identified, understood, and internalized a set of ideas to govern themselves, their relationships, their standards, and their ambitions.

The hard part, of course, is not understanding your how; it's practicing your how.

WHAT I HAVE LEARNED ABOUT LEADERSHIP

1. Be self-aware. Exercise your strengths for scale and scope. Limit your weaknesses. Ask for help when you need it.

2. Values transcend everything. Live them fully.

3. Human capital drives financial capital. (Thank you, Mr. O'Brien!)

4. Create, communicate, and achieve great goals. Bring people together around a few great goals.

5. Inspiring leadership is a contagious disease. Excitement and goose bumps work better than fear and anxiety, although all are contagious.

6. Drive positive feedback. It too can be inspiring.

7. Focus on creating the right rules (policies, procedures, structures) for an organization or culture to thrive.

8. Simplify everything that you can while seeing the whole.

9. Foster shared responsibility. It's almost never one person who is the point of failure. It's never, or almost never, one person's fault.

10. Control structure; let people do their best and express themselves. (Thank you, Marvin Weisbord and Warren Bennis!)

11. Always intervene at the right place in the system.

12. Always focus on dignity, respect, and community. (Thank you again, Marvin!)

13. It's all about mindsets. Work hard to create the best picture of reality. It's never what you perceive.

14. Leaders create change. Find the lever to create the biggest change for the least amount of effort and pull it.

15. Do the math. It tells the truth until it doesn't. There is always more to the story than just the numbers.

16. Number-based parameters (e.g., cut 10 percent) are simple decisions that don't work.

17. Think, think, and think it through again. (Think thrice, act once!)

18. Take big consequential decisions in small bites. Take small consequential decisions in big bites.

19. Attack delays in a process or system. Delays always cost you big.

20. Always be discarding. Don't cling to your successes or hang on to things because of legacy.

21. Create transparency .

22. It's always about putting the right people together. Always!

23. Heroes and heroic behavior tell you a lot about what's wrong in your system.

24. Always look at the whole, not just the parts.

25. Find the unspoken. Say it out loud.

26. Whenever possible, allow self-organizing to occur.

LEADERSHIP PROBE

Ask yourself:

- Do I truly see myself as a leader?

- Do I have enough confidence to put my name into consideration to lead when the opportunity I want arises?

- Do I have the "fire" to lead?

- Do I truly understand my capabilities as a leader, not just as an expert in the work?

- Do I have the courage and the commitment to pursue my goals even when there is disagreement, ambivalence, resistance, and outright conflict?

- Do I have the courage to do the right thing?

- Do I understand how to inspire, engage, and organize people around an innovative goal?

- Do I act in ways that are consistent with my values and my leadership principles?

- Do I understand and want to build an organization capable of achieving great goals?

EPILOGUE

Pull the string, and it will follow wherever you wish. Push it, and it will
go nowhere at all.

—Dwight D. Eisenhower, U.S. President (1953–1961)

It would be impossible, even negligent, to conclude this book without rolling the clock forward 15 years to give you some insight into
where James, Priya, and Jane have ended up in their leadership
journeys to date. When I first met all three of these leaders, purposeful leadership was not even a concept. I was James's executive
coach in a leadership development program in which he was a participant. I was Priya's boss's executive coach when I first met her.
He thought she was the most talented leader and builder he had
ever seen. I met Jane at Linkage's Global Institute of Leadership
Development when I facilitated her and the peers from her organization in what is known as a learning team. After the Institute, we
struck up an informal coaching relationship.

No leader is ever perfect, and most leaders go through a mul-
tidecade learning process that molds, shapes, trains, and develops

their leadership instincts and behaviors. Over time they learn to master themselves, a team, a function, then multiple functions, and finally an entire organization. They build a toolbox of skills, a set of leadership principles, followers, a style, and a sense of their own unique purpose as a leader. They start to understand they truly represent the past, are the architects of the future, and are the implementers of today as they come to understand their value as a leader, and they learn how to bring that value to fruition.

JAMES: KNOWING AND LIVING HIS PURPOSE

James was a good but not a great student. He came from a loving family who sincerely believed in him. James was extremely grateful for both the size and the closeness of his family and relatives, and he felt that he had learned a great many lessons from them. In particular, he had strong memories of his father's agreeable and kind style. His father was always in charge of everything but was always laughing and enjoying the people he surrounded himself with in whatever he did. James often referred to a particularly strong memory he had of his father leading a big charity auction ball. It was a gown and tuxedo event with millions of dollars of prizes being auctioned. James and his brothers were volunteers for the night. In his memory, James could still see his father laughing and enjoying the people, the volunteers in particular. No matter the stress, the problem, or the pressure, his father referred to everyone by name, had a kind word if not a funny but respectful saying, and had really good relationships. James learned a lot from his early years:

- Nice is an important part of life.

- Always be improving.

- Do things together; it is more fun.

- Be respectful.

- Know your stuff.

- The most important thing in your life is love.

James brought these ideas to the workplace with him, and as time went on, he found himself concentrating more and more on "always be improving" and "know your stuff." After being promoted, along with two other people, to a position where he reported directly to the chief marketing officer at a Fortune 100 company, James was asked to attend a yearlong leadership development training program.

After going through a 360-degree feedback activity, several exercises involving group work and feedback, and some lectures by members of the senior team on how they lead, James was asked to write his principles of leadership. He stuttered and he stalled. He was not happy having to write out his principles of leadership. As a practice, it seemed a waste of time to him. He resisted and he procrastinated. When the facilitators of his cohort started to catch on, they stepped in and provided some coaching.

James eventually broke down and engaged. The facilitators and program participants started by asking James about his "roots" as a leader. Where did he come from as a leader? Who were his most important role models—good and bad? Why marketing? Why this industry? What lessons as a leader had he really internalized? What was he committed to do differently because he felt things weren't working? There was a painful insight that he might be disappointing his father with the way that he was leading. As you might imagine, the program flooded his mind with memories of his father.

What inspired him? What did he believe inspired others who worked for him? Where was he right? Where was he wrong? What traditions did he love? What one thing was he so committed to, so believing of, that he would be willing to lose his job over it? And the grilling continued with, "What do you want to be as a leader of your organization? What are you willing to commit to practicing?"

James was at a crossroads, and he knew it. To his credit he dug deep and did the work of reflecting on his purpose and becoming vulnerable with a few key friends to get their input. The leadership development program gave him the theoretical grounding and the structure he had never had in the past. Coaching gave him the rigor he had not experienced when working on his own issues. He was very rigorous with external issues like spreadsheets and marketing programs. It was the reflection that allowed him to look at all his experience, draw conclusions, and go back to his role with renewed energy.

I got to be James's coach over the next two years, and his growth as a leader was exponential. He stopped relying on spreadsheets, numbers, and analytical thinking. He started to see the role visions and goals play in energizing a group of people. He learned to speak to large groups in his operation and in other operations. He came back and taught at the leadership development course with the next cohort. It wasn't too much longer he met someone who shortly became his wife. His contemporaries were astonished at the overall change in his presence. Unfortunately, when the executive vice president of marketing retired, James did not win the promotion. The leadership executives did not feel he was as broad in marketing as he needed to be, and they gave him appropriate positive feedback for his growth, incentivized him to gain more experience in a broader set of marketing and enterprise issues, and set his expectations positively. To James's credit, he was motivated by this set of events. So it was a shock when he resigned. He and his wife, also a marketing expert, were starting their own marketing consulting firm. James and I have spoken regularly over the last 14 years, and the firm is doing incredibly well. He and his wife focus on helping companies with their marketing analytics. He found his purpose and lives through it every day. He leads today with inspiration, engagement, and innovation. He has deliberately (purposefully) developed a supportive communication style: agreeable, complimentary, nonevaluative, challenging in a positive way, yet open and learning oriented. He continues to find issues and mistakes, but he deals with them differently than the young James did, often coming away with a stronger relationship with the person.

He is living his purpose and his principles.

PRIYA: BREAKTHROUGH

Priya had several courses during her MBA studies requiring her to dig deep and find herself in her career. She was always able to articulate the principles behind her process:

- Look at every subject from multiple perspectives and find the perspective that challenges you the most.

- Define the piece; create the scope of the project.

- Find the paradoxes and the inconsistencies you want to speak about that challenge you.

- Make it attractive, something that people will talk about.

- Experiment with each dimension of the piece to find out what works best.

Priya loved creating and loved the process of creating. It didn't matter what she was creating; she loved finding something in the way the land and building came together that at the same time challenged people and attracted people.

Priya was compelled to rethink her leadership when out of the blue the CEO of her organization called her up and asked her if she would like to lead—be the president of—another subsidiary. She would be the first female president in the organization's enterprise; she would be the first woman on the global executive team; and she would have a full go-to-market, operational, and support staff to lead.

The CEO was committed to supporting her, but before she could be appointed, she would need to go through a vetting process with the board of directors. To start the process, he asked her to write four separate essays for the board, answering these questions:

1. How would she govern the organization?

2. How would she lead the executive team?

3. How would she build and shape the culture of the organization?

4. How would she go about the process (a road map) of creating value for shareholders?

Priya was to become president of the enterprise's only environmental services company. She would be leaving behind design and building construction and taking on a much more demanding and challenging part of the engineering world. The CEO asked her to take a month, talk to people in the division, ask some tough questions, and see what people were thinking and feeling. In giving her a bit more of a guideline, he said that each essay should be no more than a page, to keep it simple. He also told her about a book he was reading that talked about 10X thinking and asked her to think about the question: How could we grow the business by a factor of 10 and profits by a factor of 10? As he preferred to do with every division, he would ask several board members to accompany him in a review of the division every three months. So she should be prepared for a full, one-day total business unit review every three months, and they would be reviewing her leadership principles as their primary way of looking at the whole organization.

The rest of the story moves quickly. Priya went through the assessment process, wrote her essays, was interviewed by the board, and was confirmed as the president of the Environmental Services subsidiary. It was eight months later that the entire organization was acquired by another firm. She had made a number of changes that were beginning to show up in the financials, but there was a long way to go. That didn't matter, though, since the acquiring company swept out the entire management team, including Priya.

Not one to sit still, Priya formed her own engineering consultancy and started taking projects almost within the week of being terminated. She also began a job search seeking out the presidency of a firm. Although opportunities presented themselves almost immediately, Priya declined many of them. Interestingly, an entrepreneur came along and made Priya an offer: He wanted Priya to research and propose a new and unique engineering firm.

Three proposals and many discussions later, Priya found herself the CEO of an engineering design firm of her making. She would own 49 percent of the firm. Four years later, after tremendous success, the firm was acquired by another engineering firm on the West Coast. Again, she was out of work, but she reopened her own consultancy.

Nine years later, Priya and her consultancy are both extremely successful. She not only does multiple projects a year; she is highly sought after by her city's government as an expert in doing design and in guiding the future of the city. As a result, she is also consulting for many other cities about the future of their building and construction. She has even testified before the U.S. Congress.

Priya has been through too many acquisitions in her career. It was inevitable that she open her own firm, particularly after having created and sold a successful start-up. She is still a networker extraordinaire, a consummate artist in her preparation, a mentor to many young women that she brings into her firm to intern and work, and a passionate lover of great building design.

JANE: DILIGENT DISCIPLINE

Jane was always the professional. She understood her "how" as the workerlike practice of always being prepared, always having alternatives, and always communicating as quickly and thoroughly as possible. Jane always felt as if she had missed her calling when she didn't go to law school. She always saw herself as the calm center of a storm. She constantly toyed with the idea of being inspiring as a leader. It was a game for her until one day at lunch when her new boss asked her, "What is it that guides you as a leader?"

Jane instantly responded to her boss, "The company's mission, of course." In her words, "It was fortunate that he didn't accept that answer." Instead, he went on to tell Jane that her call center was chaotic. He added "that an organization is a reflection of its leader." He asked her to take three months and examine her operation from every angle. And he wanted her to examine herself in the process. He said he hoped that she would begin to see all the things that were invisible to her today. Further, as he got up from the lunch table, he said, "I hope that you'll find a new way to plan things out, engage the organization, and create some new practices for both the organization and yourself."

Jane took up the challenge. A somewhat forced path, but a positive, professional one nonetheless. First, she sought out the counsel of an executive coach. As they engaged, Jane put together three teams of trusted individuals in her organization: a process team, an outcomes team, and an organizational team. She asked each team for an assessment of current reality, an assessment of what could or should be, and two lists: What needs to change about our organization? What can or should remain the same about our organization? In addition, she asked each team for a report card on her leadership, warning the teams that she had a refined HMD (horse manure detector). She promised to stay open, ask questions, and not shoot the messenger.

In the first six weeks, the teams combined and recombined and re-sorted their respective missions, ultimately creating one big team. As a team, they attended a leadership institute (GILD) and spent a week reflecting on themselves, each other, and the data. It took another four to five weeks for real work to get done, but Jane had her assessment. While the assessment was largely positive, it was evident she needed to figure out who she was as a leader. She sat down with her coach, and they did the work of looking at Jane, her purpose, and her principles of leadership. The assessment had really emphasized two major issues with her leadership style: She was disempowering and not systemic or holistic in her thinking.

To help her decide what to do, Jane and her coach posed several questions: (1) Will change bring benefits? (2) What will be the worst-case scenario of going through a change in leadership style? (3) Will people respond to the change? And (4) How do I not let the organization go backward as I try to change?

In the end, she decided to muster the courage and go forward with a change. This was a change that would require Jane to develop her capacity for self-awareness as well as self-development. Her confidence in her ability to deliver results the way she was leading was matched by her absolute fear of losing control and having results drift in the wrong direction. Even more confusing to her, she did not connect an improvement in her self-awareness with anything particularly useful. She found it hard to understand how changing her self-awareness could impact a gigantic call center operation. Nevertheless, she set out to define her purpose and her principles and to lead by them. And to no one's surprise, it didn't go so well at first. Changing habits and letting go of control was harder and messier than she had ever imagined. And to make matters worse, the organization had all sorts of story lines about what was going on with Jane. But like the proud sponsor and mentor that he was, her boss was supportive and happy with everything that was happening.

Like James, Jane found many unexplained benefits in her growing self-awareness. A part of her life that she had completely ignored suddenly become a major part of her life: She found a life partner, her husband, and with her life partner she found friends, community, and a charity that she deeply cared about and joined the board of directors. At work, after six or seven rough months, the baseline performance of the call center jumped uncharacteristically. And it continued to outperform itself. And while it took several years and she didn't get the COO role, Jane was eventually promoted to executive vice president of administration. She was the senior leader in charge of human resources, facilities, security, the daycare center, community relations, and the company's foundation and charitable giving, as well as the company's diversity and inclusion efforts. She had become great at getting everyone to understand the problem and collectively understand and be aware of how they were each contributing to the problem. She had stopped all her bad habits, built a great team, and kept the team members organized and innovating. The new norm in her organization was a new norm every few months. She was confidently navigating her membership on the executive team, her new role was going extraordinarily well, and she had a life outside work. As a leader, she had become focused and purposeful, and she avoided simple explanations of the complex, kept the big picture in mind, and had learned how to not overcontrol. Jane achieved a comfort in her own skin as a leader. Within her company, she is beloved and respected and is the leader that everyone wants as a mentor or sponsor.

PRINCIPLES EVOLVE

It's important to understand that leadership is an active profession and requires as much professional practice as any other. While anyone with any style can lead, evolution and enhancement should be part of a leader's discipline as the leader builds leadership muscle, handles difficult situations, and grows a presence. Evolution and enhancement are an inevitable part of becoming a more purposeful leader.

James, Priya, and Jane have become purposeful leaders. I am inspired by them every day. They and others like them are my mission.

PRINCIPLES PROBE

- Where did you come from as a leader?

- Who are your most important role models—good and bad?

- Why did you choose this company?

- Why did you choose this industry?

- What lessons as a leader have you really internalized?

- What are you committed to do differently because things are not working? What can you say is directly caused by your involvement or lack of involvement?

- What inspires you?

- What do you believe inspires others who work for you?

- Where are you right?

- Where are you wrong?

- What traditions in your organization do you love? Or what traditions would you love to see?

- What one thing are you so committed to, so believing of, that you would be willing to lose your job over it?

- What do you want to be as a leader of your organization? What are you willing to commit to practicing?

- What's your plan for when you're tempted to break your principles?

REFERENCES AND FURTHER READING

Engage

AUTHORS: Deborah Ancona, Thomas W. Malone, Wanda J. Orlikowski, and Peter M. Senge
CITATION: Ancona, D., Malone, T. W., Orlikowski, W. J., and Senge, P. M. (2007). "In Praise of the Incomplete Leader." *Harvard Business Review*, 85(2), 92–100.

AUTHORS: Marc H. Anderson and Peter Y. T. Sun
CITATION: Anderson, M. H., and Sun, P. Y. (2015). "Reviewing Leadership Styles: Overlaps and the Need for a New 'Full-Range Theory.'" *International Journal of Management Reviews.*

AUTHOR: Peter Bregman
CITATION: Bregman, P. (2018). *Leading with Emotional Courage: How to Have Hard Conversations, Create Accountability, and Inspire Action on Your Most Important Work.* John Wiley and Sons.

AUTHOR: Brene Brown
CITATION: Brown, B. (2010). *The Gifts of Imperfection: Let Go of Who You Think You're Supposed to Be and Embrace Who You Are.* Hazelden Publishing.

AUTHOR: James MacGregor Burns
CITATION: Burns, James MacGregor (1978). *Leadership.* Harper and Row.

AUTHOR: Kim S. Cameron
CITATION: Cameron, K. S. (2012). *Positive Leadership: Strategies for Extraordinary Performance.* Barrett-Koehler Publishers.

AUTHOR: Jay A. Conger
CITATION: Conger, J. A. (1999). "Charismatic and Transformational Leadership in Organizations: An Insider's Perspective on These Developing Streams of Research." *The Leadership Quarterly*, 10(2), 145–179.

AUTHOR: Daniel Edelman
CITATION: *2019 Edelman Trust Barometer*, Edelman, 2019

AUTHORS: Robert Galford and Anne Siebold Drapeau
CITATION: Galford, R. and Drapeau, A. S. (2011). *The Trusted Leader: Bringing Out the Best in Your People and Your Company.* Atria Books.

AUTHOR: Robert K. Greenleaf
CITATION: Greenleaf, R. K. (1970). *The Servant as Leader.* Robert K. Greenleaf Publishing Center.

AUTHORS: Ronald A. Heifetz, Alexander Grashow, and Marty Linsky
CITATION: Heifetz, R., Grashow, A., and Linsky, M. (2009). *The Practice of Adaptive Leadership: Tools and Tactics for Changing Your Organization and the World.* Harvard Business Review Press.

AUTHORS: Paul Hersey and Kenneth H. Blanchard
CITATION: Hersey, P., and Blanchard, K. H. (1977). *Management of Organizational Behavior: Utilizing Human Resources.* Prentice Hall.

AUTHOR: Daniel Kahneman
CITATION: Kahneman, D. (2013). *Thinking, Fast and Slow*. Farrer, Straus, and Giroux.

AUTHORS: Robert G. Lord and Rosalie J. Hall
CITATION: Lord, R. G., and Hall, R. J. (2005). "Identity, Deep Structure and the Development of Leadership Skill." *The Leadership Quarterly*, 16(4), 591–615.

AUTHOR: Scott E. Page
CITATION: Page, S. E. (2017). The Diversity Bonus: How Great Teams Pay Off in the Knowledge Economy. Princeton University Press.

AUTHORS: John E. Tropman and Lynn Wooten
CITATION: Tropman, J. E., and Wooten, L. (2010). "Executive Leadership: a 7C Approach." *Problems and Perspectives in Management*, 8(4), 47–57.

Inspire

AUTHORS: Teresa M. Amabile and Steven J. Kramer
CITATION: Amabile, T. and Kramer, S. (2011). "The Progress Principle: Using Small Wins to Ignite Joy, Engagement, and Creativity at Work." *Harvard Business Press*.

AUTHOR: A. M. Carton
CITATION: Carton, A. M. (2018). "I'm Not Mopping Floors, I'm Putting a Man on the Moon: How NASA Leaders Enhanced the Meaningfulness of Work by Changing the Meaning of Work." *Administrative Science Quarterly*, 63(2) 323–369.

AUTHOR: Jim Collins
CITATION: Collins, J. (2001). *Good to Great: Why Some Companies Make the Leap and Others Don't*. Harper Business.

AUTHOR: Zenger Folkman
CITATION: Z. F. Folkman (2011, October 4). "The 16 Days of Competencies: #10 Inspires and Motivates Others to High Performance." Retrieved April 5, 2017, from http://zengerfolkman.com/the-16-days-of -competencies-10-inspires-and-motivates-others-to-high-performance/.

AUTHOR: Justin Menkes
CITATION: Menkes, J. (2011). *Better Under Pressure: How Great Leaders Bring Out the Best in Themselves and Others.* Harvard Business Review Press.

AUTHOR: National Research Council Canada
CITATION: Government of Canada, National Research Council. (2015, December 18). "Inspirational Leadership (Core Competency)." National Research Council Canada. Retrieved April 05, 2017, from http://www.nrc-cnrc.gc.ca/eng/careers/behavioural_competencies/ mg_inspirational_leadership.html.

AUTHORS: Nitin Nohria, Boris Groysberg, and Linda-Eling Lee
CITATION: Nohria, N., Groysberg, B., and Lee, L. E. (2008). "Employee Motivation: A Powerful New Model." *Harvard Business Review*, 86(7/8), 78–84.

AUTHOR: Simon Sinek
CITATION: Sinek, S. (2011). *Start With Why: How Great Leaders Inspire Everyone to Take Action.* Portfolio.

AUTHOR: Simon Sinek
CITATION: Sinek, S. (2017). *Find Your Why: A Practical Guide for Discovering Purpose for You and Your Team.* Portfolio.

AUTHORS: James W. Sipe and Don M. Frick
CITATION: Sipe, J. W. and Frick, D. M. (2009). *Seven Pillars of Servant Leadership: Practicing the Wisdom of Leading by Serving.* Paulist Press.

AUTHOR: Dave Ulrich
CITATION: Ulrich, D. (2009). *The Leadership Code: Five Rules to Lead By.* Harvard Business Review Press.

AUTHORS: Jasmine Vergauwe, Bart Wille, Joeri Hofmans, Robert B. Kaiser, and Filip De Fruyt
CITATION: Vergauwe, J., Wille, B., Hofmans, J., Kaiser, R. B., and De Fruyt, F. (2018.) "The Double-Edged Sword of Leader Charisma: Understanding the Curvilinear Relationship Between Charismatic Personality and Leader Effectiveness." *Journal of Personality and Social Psychology* 114 (1): 110–130.

Innovate

AUTHORS: Joanna Barsh, Marla M. Capozzi, and Jonathan Davidson
CITATION: Barsh, J., Capozzi, M. M., and Davidson, J. (2008). "Leadership and Innovation." *McKinsey Quarterly*, 1, 36.

AUTHORS: Larry Bossidy, Ram Charan, and Charles Burck
CITATION: Bossidy, L., Charan, R., and Burck, C. (2011). *Execution: The Discipline of Getting Things Done.* Random House.

AUTHORS: Abraham Carmeli, Ravit Meitar, and Jacob Weisberg
CITATION: Carmeli, A., Meitar, R., and Weisberg, J. (2006). "Self-Leadership Skills and Innovative Behavior at Work." *International Journal of Manpower*, 27(1), 75–90.

AUTHOR: Peter F. Drucker
CITATION: Drucker, P. (1996). *The Executive in Action: Managing for Results; Innovation and Entrepreneurship;* and *The Effective Executive.* Harper Business.

AUTHOR: Jim Harter
CITATION: Harter, J. (2016). *First, Break All the Rules: What the World's Greatest Managers Do Differently.* Gallup Press.

AUTHORS: Linda A. Hill, Maurizio Travaglini, Greg Brandeau, and Emily Stecker
CITATION: Hill, L.A., Travaglini, M., Brandeau, G., and Stecker, E. (2010). "Unlocking the Slices of Genius in Your Organization: Leading for Innovation." In N. Nohria and R. Khurana (eds.), *Handbook of Leadership Theory and Practice: An HBS Centennial Colloquium on Advancing Leadership.* Boston, MA: Harvard Business School Publishing Corporation, 611–654.

AUTHOR: Jane M. Howell
CITATION: Howell, J. M. (2005). "The Right Stuff: Identifying and Developing Effective Champions of Innovation." *The Academy of Management Executive,* 19(2), 108–119.

AUTHORS: A. Walter, K.P. Parboteeah, F. Riesenhuber, and M. Hoegl
CITATION: Walter, A., Parboteeah, K. P., Riesenhuber, F., and Hoegl, M. (2011). "Championship Behaviors and Innovations Success: An Empirical Investigation of University Spin-Offs." *Journal of Product Innovation Management,* 28(4), 586–598.

Achieve

AUTHOR: Bernard M. Bass
CITATION: Bass, B. M. (1985). *Leadership and Performance Beyond Expectation.* New York: Free Press.

AUTHOR: John Doerr
CITATION: Doerr, J. (2018). *Measure What Matters.* Portfolio Publishers.

AUTHORS: Hubert L. Dreyfus and Stuart E. Dreyfus
CITATION: Dreyfus, H. L. and Dreyfus, S. E. (1986). *Mind Over Machine.* New York: The Free Press.

AUTHORS: Alice H. Eagly and Blair T. Johnson
CITATION: Eagly, A. H., and Johnson, B. T. (1990). "Gender and Leadership Style: A Meta-Analysis." *Psychological Bulletin,* 108(2), 233.

AUTHOR: Malcom Gladwell
CITATION: Gladwell, M. (2007). *Blink: The Power of Thinking Without Thinking.* Back Bay Books.

AUTHOR: Seth Godin
CITATION: Godin, S. (2008). *Tribes: We Need You to Lead Us.* Portfolio.

AUTHOR: G. Graen
CITATION: Graen, G. (1976). "Role-Making Processes of Leadership Development." In M. D. Dunnette (ed.), *Handbook of Industrial and Organizational Psychology.* Chicago: Rand McNally, 1201–1245.

AUTHOR: Michael Lewis
CITATION: Lewis, M. (2004). *Moneyball: The Art of Winning an Unfair Game.* W. W. Norton & Company.

AUTHORS: Noam Wasserman, Bharat Anand, and Nitin Nohria
CITATION: Wasserman, N., Bharat, A., and Nohria, N. (2010). "When Does Leadership Matter? A Contingent Opportunities View of CEO Leadership." In N. Nohria and R. Khurana (Eds.) *Handbook of Leadership Theory and Practice: An HBS Centennial Colloquium on Advancing Leadership.* Boston, MA: Harvard Business School Publishing Corporation, 27–63.

AUTHORS: Steve Zaffron and Dave Logan
CITATION: Zaffron, S., and Logan, D. (2012). *The Three Laws of Performance: Rewriting the Future of Your Organization and Your Life.* Read How You Want Publishers.

Become

AUTHOR: The Arbinger Institute
CITATION: Arbinger Institute. (2012). *Leadership and Self-Deception: Getting Out of the Box.* ReadHowYouWant.

AUTHOR: Warren Bennis
CITATION: Bennis, W. (1989). *On Becoming a Leader.* Addison-Wesley Pub. Co.

AUTHORS: Warren Bennis and Burton Nanus
CITATION: Bennis, W., and Nanus, B. (1985). *Leaders: Strategies for Taking Charge.* Harper and Row.

AUTHOR: Susan Mackenty Brady
CITATION: Brady, S. M. (2019). *Mastering Your Inner Critic and 7 Other High Hurdles to Advancement: How the Best Women Leaders Practice Self-Awareness to Change What Really Matters.* McGraw-Hill Education.

AUTHOR: Brene Brown
CITATION: Brown, B. (2018). *Dare to Lead. Brave Work. Tough Conversations. Whole Hearts.* Penguin Random House UK.

AUTHOR: Peter F. Drucker
CITATION: Drucker, P. (2017). *Managing Oneself.* Harvard Business Review Press.

AUTHORS: Janet M. Dukerich, Mary Lippitt Nichols, Dawn R. Elm, and David A. Vollrath
CITATION: Dukerich, J. M., Nichols, M. L., Elm, D. R., and Vollrath, D. A. (1990). "Moral Reasoning in Groups: Leaders Make a Difference." *Human Relations,* 43(5), 473–493.

AUTHOR: Tasha Eurich
CITATION: Eurich, T. (2017). *Insight: Why We're Not as Self-Aware as We Think, and How Seeing Ourselves Clearly Helps Us Succeed at Work and in Life.* Crown Publishers.

AUTHOR: Fred E. Fiedler
CITATION: Fiedler, F. E. (1963). *A Contingency Model of Leadership Effectiveness.* Group Effectiveness Research Laboratory, University of Illinois.

AUTHORS: John Gerzema and Michael D'Antonio
CITATION: Gerzema, J. and D'Antonio, M. (2013) *The Athena Doctrine: How Women (and the Men Who Think Like Them) Will Rule the Future.* Jossey-Bass.

AUTHOR: Bill George
CITATION: George, B. (2003). *Authentic Leadership.* Wiley Press.

AUTHOR: Marshall Goldsmith
CITATION: Goldsmith, M. (2007). *What Got You Here Won't Get Your There.* Hachette Books.

AUTHORS: Sean T. Hannah, Bruce J. Avolio, and Fred O. Walumbwa
CITATION: Hannah, S. T., Avolio, B. J., and Walumbwa, F. O. (2011). "Relationships Between Authentic Leadership, Moral Courage, and Ethical and Pro-Social Behaviors." *Business Ethics Quarterly*, 21(04), 555–578.

AUTHORS: Erika Hayes James and Lynn Perry Wooten
CITATION: James, E. H. & Wooten, L. P. (2010). *Leading Under Pressure: From Surviving to Thriving Before, During, and After a Crisis.* Routledge.

AUTHORS: Frances Hesselbein, M. Goldsmith, and Sarah McArthur
CITATION: Hesselbein, F., Goldsmith, M. & McArthur, S. (2018). *Work is Love Made Visible: Finding Your Purpose from the World's Greatest Thought Leaders.* Wiley.

AUTHOR: Linda A. Hill
CITATION: Hill, L. A. (2019) *Becoming a Manager: How New Managers Master the Challenges of Leadership.* Harvard Review Press.

AUTHORS: R. J. House and T. R. Mitchell
CITATION: House, R. J., and Mitchell, T. R. (1974) "Path-Goal Theory of Leadership." *Journal of Contemporary Business*, 3, 81–97.

AUTHOR: Herminia Ibarra
CITATION: Ibarra, H. (2015). *Act Like a Leader, Think Like a Leader.* Harvard Business Review Press.

AUTHORS: D. A. Kenny and S. J. Zaccaro
CITATION: Kenny, D. A., and Zaccaro, S. J. (1983). "An Estimate of Variance Due to Traits in a Leader." *Journal of Applied Psychology.*

AUTHOR: Nannerl O. Keohane
CITATION: Keohane, N. O. (2010) *Thinking About Leadership.* Princeton University Press.

AUTHOR: Malcolm Shepherd Knowles
CITATION: Knowles, M. S. (1970). *The Modern Practice of Adult Education: Andragogy Versus Pedagogy.* New York: Association Press.

AUTHOR: Tom Kolditz
CITATION: Kolditz, Tom. (2010) *In Extremis Leadership: Leading As If Your Life Depended On It.* Jossey-Bass.

AUTHORS: James M. Kouzes and Barry, M. Posner
CITATION: Kouzes, J. M. and Posner, M. (2016). *Learning Leadership: The Five Fundamentals of Becoming an Exemplary Leader.* Wiley.

AUTHORS: James M. Kouzes and Barry Z. Posner
CITATION: Kouzes, J. M. and Posner, B. Z. (2010). *The Truth About Leadership: The No-Fads, Heart-of-the-Matter Facts You Need to Know.* Jossey-Bass.

AUTHOR: Richard J. Leider
CITATION: Leider, R. J. (2015). *The Power of Purpose: Find Meaning, Live Longer, Better.* Third Edition. Barrett-Koehler Publishers.

AUTHOR: R. D. Mann
CITATION: Mann, R. D. (1959). "A Review of the Relationships Between Personality and Performance in Small Groups." *Psychological Bulletin,* 56(4), 241–270.

AUTHORS: R. R. McCrae and O. P. John
CITATION: McCrae, R. R., and John, O. P. (1992) "An Introduction to the Five-Factor Model and Its Applications." *Journal of Personality,* 60, 175–215.

AUTHOR: Justin Menkes
CITATION: Menkes, J. (2009). *Executive Intelligence: What All Great Leaders Have.* HarperCollins ebooks.

AUTHORS: Nitin Nohria and Rakesh Khurana
CITATION: Nohria, N. and Khurana, R. (2010). *Handbook of Leadership Theory and Practice.* Harvard Business Review Press.

AUTHOR: William J. O'Brien
CITATION: O'Brien, W. J. (2008). *Character at Work: Building Prosperity Through The Practice of Virtue.* Paulist Press.

AUTHOR: Michelle Obama
CITATION: Obama, M. (2018). *Becoming.* Crown Publishing Group.

AUTHOR: Daniel Pink
CITATION: Pink, D. (2009). *Drive: The Surprising Truth About What Motivates Us.* Riverhead Books.

AUTHOR: W. C. H. Prentice
CITATION: Prentice, W. C. H. (January, 2004) *Understanding Leadership.* Harvard Business Review.

AUTHOR: Terry L. Price
CITATION: Price, T. L. (2008). *Leadership Ethics: An Introduction.* Cambridge University Press.

AUTHOR: Tom Rath
CITATION: Rath, T. (2009) *Strengths Based Leadership: Great Leaders, Teams, and Why People Follow.* Gallup Press.

AUTHOR: Donald Sull
CITATION: Sull, D. (June, 2003). "Managing by Commitments." *Harvard Business Review.*

AUTHORS: Dave Ulrich, N. Smallwood, and K. Sweetman
CITATION: Ulrich, D., Smallwood, N., and Sweetman, K. (2015). *The Leadership Capital Index.* Barrett-Koehler Publishers.

AUTHORS: Dave Ulrich and Norm Smallwood

CITATION: Ulrich, D., and Smallwood, N. (2006) *How Leaders Build Value: Using People, Organization, and Other Intangibles to Get Bottom-Line Results.* Wiley.

INDEX

ABOUT THE AUTHOR

MARK HANNUM is the Chief Research Officer at Linkage. He partners with clients to create better business and organizational results. An organizational development consultant by training, Mark has focused on understanding and improving executive processes and decision making. Through his work with executive teams, leadership teams, and shared services organizations, his clients have credited him with helping them manage through difficult risks, improve business operations, lead and coach through acquisitions and integrations, and take advantage of growth opportunities.

Become is Mark's debut as an author.